CW01081588

ABOUT THE BOOK

There's hardly anything more delightful for a horse lover than watching horses move freely and easily—whether they are playing in a pasture or working under a rider. Such movement can be proof of equestrian skill of the highest order: the horse trustingly and joyfully cooperates with his rider and completely accepts the aids. Sadly, in our dressage arenas we often see quite a different picture: misguided ambition or simple ignorance forces young horses into a frame that may cause long-lasting damage to their health. Many of the riders, trainers, and top athletes responsible for this may claim that they train according to "Classical Principles," but unfortunately, their methods are *not* always guided by true horse sense and classical training principles. So how can riders and lovers of the sport recognize which training methods damage horses in the long run, and which have the horse's health and well-being in mind?

This book answers this question and provides arguments for what is actually "right" and "wrong." The title of the book, *Tug of War*, is deliberately provocative because author Dr. Gerd Heuschmann—an experienced equine veterinarian–openly confronts developments in dressage—as a sport and a recreational pastime–that he asserts have taken a wrong turn. The book's purpose, however, is not simply to lament the situation. Drawing on basic anatomical and physiological knowledge, Dr. Heuschmann proves how incorrect riding has a negative effect on the horse's health. He then clarifies why it's worthwhile to train your horse according to time-proven, Classical Principles.

Where does this road lead?

PUBLIC LETTER

Dear FN, FEI, and German Association of Judges,

Where will this road lead us?

A very successful, and maybe the most impressive World Equestrian Games yet was held in 2006. Dressage horses producing extremely "expressive" rides were awarded high marks and medals. Now that our impressions are over a year old I would like to pose several questions to the heads of equestrian organizations. Since your opinions are influential, is this way of riding, highly praised by judges, really what you would like to promote? Can you, in good conscience, call what we saw "classical training" of the horse? Are you satisfied with the work of our highest level dressage judges?

I seem to remember a wonderful horse, which according to the 50,000 audience members should have won the competition. The team of judges came very close to satisfying everyone's wish. For me, and I'm not the only one, there are still several large questions looming over this horse's results. This sensational horse didn't fulfill one single criterion of classical training. The rhythm was not maintained in any of the gaits. Suppleness and relaxation didn't exist, impulsion from the hind legs was not recognizable, and a connection to the bit—in a classical sense—could not be identified. Every moment of suspension was developed from a tense back. A correct passage was never shown. The hind legs were simply pulled under the horse's belly and held for a moment's hesitation. What was supposed to be piaffe, the Grand Prix movement requiring the most collection, was nearly identical to Udo Bürger's description of "pseudo-piaffe" in *The Way to Perfect Horsemanship*: a nodding head, a swishing tail held tensely, a high croup, and the horse stepping wide.

We saw a spectacular horse that presented a flashy display, but no more. The FEI judges' evaluation of this horse was, in my opinion, "bankrupt." Even the usually critical and informed magazines reported a new superstar had arrived!

How could judges at this high level let themselves be so easily deceived? Or, is this the new interpretation of classical riding? Who will have the courage—and the competence—to steer us back in the right direction?

I eagerly await your answer.

Sincerely,
Gerd Heuschmann

Dr. Gerd Heuschmann

Tug of War: Classical versus "Modern" Dressage

Why Classical Training Works and How Incorrect "Modern" Riding Negatively Affects Horses' Health

Translated by Reina Abelshauser

J.A. Allen • London

First published in Great Britain in 2007 by
J.A. Allen
45–47 Clerkenwell Green
London ECIR 0HT

J.A. Allen is an imprint of Robert Hale Limited

www.halebooks.com

ISBN: 978-0-85131-950-6

Revised edition 2009
Printed in China

Originally published in the German language as *Finger in der Wunde* by Wu Wei Verlag, 86938 Schondorf, Germany, 2006

A catalogue record for this book is available from the British Library

Interior design by Christine Orterer
Cover design by Heather Mansfield

10 9 8 7 6 5

DEDICATION

To my dear parents, Inge and Gerhard Heuschmann.
With great encouragement, they made it possible for my siblings
and me to take up the sport of riding. And without their support,
this book would never have been written.

I also dedicate this book to my partner, Stephanie Martens,
who supports me with unfailing commitment, and who
always finds a new way to motivate me even when
I am at the end of my tether!

CONTENTS

CONTENTS

FOREWORD BY THE AUTHOR FOR THE NEW EDITION

For the most part the biomechanics of the classical training system according to the German military riding manual *HDV 12* have not been scientifically analyzed or proven. To this day, the understanding of biomechanics in classical teaching is still based on empirical knowledge. Experienced riders and trainers with in-depth anatomical knowledge first discussed this in the 1939 work *The Rider Forms the Horse* by Bürger and Zeitschmann.

However, the first scientific studies failed due to the researchers' lack of riding experience. There were many attempts to measure how the head and neck position of the horse affects the quality of movement of the back but they were incorrectly evaluated. In my opinion, scientific study of this subject is a very difficult undertaking. The only way to find meaningful, objective results is to balance competent knowledge of riding with correct research methods. I would hope that future scientific efforts would be conducted under these conditions.

This revision of my book became necessary in order to address areas of contention. Additionally, I have subsequently broadened and changed my own knowledge of biomechanics based on the teachings of the classical *École de Légèreté* (school of lightness), founded by Philippe Karl in 2004. As my own skill on horseback develops, my understanding of biomechanics increases as a result. I would surmise that in addition to the *HDV 12*, there should be an equivalent manual on the teachings of the *Légèreté*. I have found it extremely valuable to think differently and to try to understand another philosophy—that of the *École de Légèreté*. This effort has brought me considerably further in my studies.

Gerd Heuschmann
Warendorf, Germany

FOREWORD BY ULRICH SCHNITZER

To train and use horses in a way that preserves their capacity and willingness to perform for a long period of time has challenged the art of riding since its birth. The evolution of this art was originally driven by military and economic needs, and later sustained by the equestrian traditions of the royal courts.

In the first decades of the twentieth century, the German military riding manual *HDV 12*, a summary of military knowledge and experience about training horses in a horse-friendly way was compiled. From this concise document (which, it should be noted, was accepted and acknowledged by those in the competitive scene) evolved the FN manual, the generally valid guideline for the sport of riding and training horses today.

Advancements in military technology and times of relative peace meant horses were soon mainly used for sport and pleasure. The breeding industry reacted to these developments and now produces horses possessing conformation and a rideability that the great riders of the past could only dream of. With these top horses, highly qualified riders and trainers produce performances on a scale that would have been previously unimaginable. Yet, this success must not blind us to the fact that—especially in the discipline of dressage—we see patterns of movement and physical postures in the horses (even among the very best equine athletes) that indicate the use of harmful training methods. If a horse is highly talented, it can be tempting to force or accelerate his training. Sadly, more and more people seem to believe that the "old way" of training a horse, which requires spending a greater amount of time on the basics, is outmoded. Meanwhile, the horse's physiology, anatomy, and biomechanics haven't changed.

This is where Dr. Heuschmann's work begins. As a practicing veterinarian and experienced rider he's confronted with the consequences of incorrect training every day. Much of his time away from work is spent informing riders and instructors through lectures and clinics. His book follows up on Bürger and Zietzschmann's *The Rider Forms the Horse,* which provided scientific support for the German principles of riding at the end of the 1930s. Like them, Dr. Heuschmann neatly explains physiological and anatomical relationships and identifies the injurious consequences of employing incorrect methods.

This book is an appeal to riders to use gentle training methods; to judges to sharpen their eyes to recognize unnatural or forced motion sequences and evaluate them accordingly; to national and international organizations to review their regulations; and to spectators to reject spectacular presentations if the methods used to obtain them are not horse-friendly.

Dr. Heuschmann's book belongs in the hands of everyone who is involved in training or caring for horses in any way.

Prof. Dr.-Ing. Ulrich Schnitzer
Karlsruhe, Germany

FOREWORD BY PETER KUNZMANN

Dr. Gerd Heuschmann presents a book that says important things about animal ethics—namely that creatures that are sentient have to be protected from harm to their well-being for their own sake. The author evaluates developments in equestrian sport and arrives at his conclusions and recommendations with conviction. At the heart of the matter lies the belief that *the horse* is the decisive factor that must determine how a rider, trainer, or owner chooses to act or not act.

In essence, this is what Dr. Heuschmann believes: "*The horse* and all its natural and potential predispositions determines the tempo and character of its training—*not* the human being." Here he refers (and rightfully so) to one of the "Ethical Principles for the True Horseman" published as *Die Ethische Grundsätze des Pferdefreundes* by the German National Equestrian Federation (FN), which state: *The use of the horse in competition as well as in general riding, driving and vaulting must be geared toward the horse's ability, temperament and willingness to perform. Manipulating a horse's capacity to work by means of medication or other "horse-unfriendly" influences should be rejected by all and people engaged in such practices should be prosecuted* (see p. 127 for complete list).

In terms of animal ethics, such demands would seem to be a matter of course, and yet they are not really that commonplace. This book provides the reader with the technical knowledge and understanding of horses and horsemanship necessary to conscientiously choose them as the guiding principles. Only the person who possesses thorough equine knowledge can appropriately adjust his actions to suit a horse's nature and physicality, while at the same time promoting its healthy development—an important issue that Dr. Heuschmann emphatically insists be given time and space. He thereby uses his extensive knowledge to serve the estimable purpose of establishing educated, "competent" interaction with these animals.

Dr. Heuschmann also contributes to something that has been—and still is—debated in animal ethics under the label "animal dignity." It goes beyond questions regarding mere animal welfare; it is about having insights into each animal's own intrinsic value and individual nature, and respecting it. The animal's nature should be allowed to "unfold," and this unfolding must not be obstructed, prevented, or broken by mankind's demands and power over it. The book also teaches us, page after page, to see horses first and foremost as horses, and then (and only then) as the status symbols, breeding successes, or financial assets they might also be.

In a world dominated by performance-oriented and commercialized riding—the very kind criticized by Dr. Heuschmann—these postulations may rub salt into wounds. Individuals addressed might possibly protest. They should, however, take a closer look as it is actually in their own interest to do so. In western industrial societies, attention to animal welfare has grown rapidly, and animal-rights activists will turn a critical eye onto equestrian sport—and they will be quick to vocalize critique if conditions they feel are not animal-friendly are apparent. As well, the great respect that those outside the equestrian world currently have for most riders, trainers, and owners will be gambled away if serious doubts are raised regarding the welfare of horses used in competition. If this leads to a conflict, most of our non-riding contemporaries will intuitively side with the horses and against the riders, judges, or breeders. The consequences of accusations of actual or presumed "cruelty inflicted on animals" would be disastrous for everybody involved.

This alone is reason enough to take Dr. Heuschmann's allegations seriously and to engage in his "school of horse-friendly riding." It's not the most important reason—from an ethical point of view that is simply that the human being, as the "power-holder" in the relationship, owes the best possible care and respect to his animal partner.

Prof. Dr. phil. Peter Kunzmann
Friedrich-Schiller University, Jena, Germany

PREFACE

For readers in the USA and UK, and other English-speaking countries

It certainly is an undisputed fact that Europe, and Germany in particular, in the past few decades has had an enormous influence and played a decisive role in the development of equestrian sport all over the world. Both advances in breeding that are strictly based on the protection of animal rights, as well as highly sophisticated training methods, which have evolved over the past centuries, have provided Europe with an opportunity to export its philosophies and spread the art of riding to people elsewhere who admire the Europeans' aesthetically beautiful, well-trained horses.

Consequently, Europe has been exporting countless numbers of horses to fulfill a huge demand. In order to cater to this market, the horse-training process is being shortened, and many of us Europeans are forgetting about the classical, time-proven training principles. A group of trainers has evolved who strive only for the quickest way to success in the horse show business, and with it the ensuing economic reward. Such a monetary goal, in and of itself, certainly isn't something that's fundamentally wrong, however, if on the way to such success the horse is reduced to a mere object or an economic asset to be moulded only for marketing purposes, then, in my view, we enter into a situation, which from the viewpoint of animal rights is not only very dangerous but also morally questionable.

Some horses are being trained with mechanical and technical devices in the shortest time possible. In other words, being trained mechanically. Other nations with little historical understanding of the classical development of riding and horse sports, are attempting to emulate these quick training methods, and inevitably, one of the means of producing such horses—"hand-dominated" riding—is also being copied.

Sadly, riders and trainers in a horse-importing nation like the United States are widely imitating this procedure, and this is happening despite the fact that hand- and strength-dominated riding isn't part of the American way of riding at all. Just remember all the reputable jumper riders who demonstrated to the world a wonderfully light and horse-friendly riding style! And, consider that it's an American, Melissa Simms, living part-time in Germany and working from the Von Neindorff Riding Institute, who is showing the entire equestrian world that riding with feel and delicacy in harmony with the horse also leads to great success.

During my last 20 years as a practicing veterinarian, I've learned some things that have made me stop and think. I believe the time has come to critically analyze our sport so that we don't continue the sort of riding and training trends I've discussed in this Preface.

The goal of training should be to further the horse's capacity to perform, and optimize his physical beauty as well as his overall well-being by taking enough time. By writing this book, I'm appealing to every rider to follow this goal regardless of equestrian discipline or nationality.

So it is with this entreaty in mind that I wish all of you great success and a healthy partnership with your horses.

Gerd Heuschmann
Warendorf, Germany, June 2007

ABOUT THE AUTHOR

Dr. med. Vet. Gerhard "Gerd" Heuschmann (born in 1959 in Marktredwitz, Germany) grew up on his parents' agricultural farm, with horses. He was educated to become a *Pferdewirt* (professional rider and trainer who is also schooled in horse management by the FN, the German National Equestrian Federation) at the performance center for three-day eventing in Ansbach, before studying veterinary medicine in Munich. Dr. Heuschmann worked as an assistant at the surgical animal hospital in Munich, as a consultant for the FN's department of breeding, as a DOKR (German Olympic Committee for Riding)-appointed veterinarian for the Olympic driving team, and as head of the animal hospital Domäne Karthaus, before he took over an equine veterinary practice in Warendorf with his colleague, Dr. Dirk Remmler, in 1998. Since 1998, both he and Dr. Remmler have prepared the veterinary studies courses for *Pferdewirt* students at the German Riding School in Warendorf.

I

WHO'S RESPONSIBLE FOR TODAY'S TRAINING PROBLEMS?

For most horse people, one of the main reasons for having an interest in horses is the simple aesthetics of these magnificent animals. Most people spend time with horses in order to relax and enjoy just being around them, and have little interest in using them for performance or profit. For some, however, interest in success in the sport or in economic gain trumps all other sources of motivation. It seems that in today's success-oriented society, even the very reasons people initially decide to take up equestrian sport have shifted considerably. The hunt for success and recognition often doesn't allow time or space for thoughtful, quiet work with the horse and a

Misuse of draw reins: they are being used to give the neck an "arched" form. The bridle and the noseband's flash strap is adjusted much too tightly.

RIDERS

naturally oriented training process. Thus, what has developed is a bad "craft" of horse training, in which the "repairmen" (especially the veterinarians) of poorly "crafted" sport horses have become firmly established as a "necessary" part of the training team.

According to the saying, "You can't make an omelette without breaking an egg," many of today's competitive riders engage in pulling, squeezing, jerking, and more. And, since the equestrian media frequently focuses on images of high performance competitors, it then appears that such riding is exemplary for all. *This is not the case!* It's high time we raise our voices and declare war on this "push-pull" way of riding!

How could it have come to this? In answering this question, I'll briefly discuss all the major groups of people involved with dressage horses. My goal is not to point a finger at any single functional and decision-making body, nor to generally condemn an entire professional group. However, let me say this: during the past few decades, many of the people who deal with horses on a daily basis have digressed from the sport's ideals and have instead acquired a habit of looking for whatever will produce the most spectacular show. I'll try to analyze the situation we're facing and provide you with food for thought.

RIDERS

There are currently millions of "active" riders—a number comprised of people who ride for recreation, pleasure, and sport on a more or less regular basis. A small portion of these are dressage riders who deliberately steer away from organized competitive sports and conscientiously follow riding and training philosophies that are essentially "classical" in their teachings. These people are usually individualists who have developed their own interpretation of the nature of classical riding and training and often refer to French and Spanish instructors. Such training methods are generally based on principles and riding manuals published by masters during the last two centuries, for example those of François Baucher.[1]

Top: A rider with a good seat sitting well balanced. This enables the horse to carry himself naturally with his trot rhythm not disrupted and with an exemplary development of impulsion.
Bottom: The rhythm of the diagonal pairs of legs, which should be parallel, is disrupted. The horse is showing tension and his head is tilting at the poll.

[1] Baucher, François (1796–1873): French riding master who operated his own private riding school, performed at a circus for a while and trained cavalry officers. He is the author of *A Method of Horsemanship Founded upon New Principles* (Scholarly Publishing Office, University of Michigan Library, 2006)

As far as I understand their philosophies, these riders are very concerned about training their horses without using force. They often vehemently criticize competitive riding and generally reject it. Being critical is certainly appropriate; however, so far I haven't seen anyone do much better when employing this sort of "classical" training. In my experience, sadly, the representatives of such "alternative" ways of riding and training are, for the most part, very closed-minded. I am sure they have important and interesting views and training methods that might help everyone involved. I am personally convinced that there are many approaches to the correct physiological and psychological understanding of horse training, so we should talk with each other, exchange our views, and make the best of it, for the good of the horses.

I think it is just as important for riders who ride as a hobby and don't have any competitive ambitions to increase their knowledge of horses and learn to train them. In this group, the biggest potential for error—and with it the biggest risk for the horses' well-being—lies in the people's ignorance.

The best moment in a competitive rider's life!

COMPETITIVE RIDERS

Competitive dressage as a sport has grown by leaps and bounds during the last decades. More and more riders—including many beginners—want to test their ability against their competitors, prove their skills and be rewarded. Unfortunately, however, some ardent devotees to the sport lack the necessary knowledge and skills. They scan through the calendar pages published by the various riding and breeding associations looking for competition dates to put together a full schedule of events. For these riders, participating in shows has become the main purpose of their hobby, and their horses have become a means to serve this purpose. The real task of a rider, which is to train a horse, has taken a back seat. As a consequence, more and more horses develop health problems because they're used incorrectly or are trained with the use of force. The steadily rising number of equine veterinarians and hospitals are proof of this development.

One pays a high price for the achievements gained in the show ring, at the horse's expense.

The riders, however, are not the only ones to be blamed for this situation—they are only part of a development in which others, especially judges and officials, play a decisive role as well.

BREEDERS

BREEDERS

Applying strict criteria and a careful selection process, a large number of breeders have been trying for decades to provide exceptional stud horses and fantastic riding horses, which give the impression of being able to produce spectacular gaits without any effort—even seem ready for competition—at a young age without having received any training. Some riders are blinded by the apparent potential of these well-bred horses, and believe that they only have to get on and win ribbons when they enter the show ring with this kind of "horse material." Some breeders don't do much to change this way of thinking for the following reason: *the greater the rider's desire to be successful, the more the economic pressures, the more he will force the training of their horses.* Sadly, young horses, in particular, become mere objects of profit, and are often not ridden and trained in a way that is appropriate for their age. After all, "time is money." In our current system, taking the time—the years—needed to train a young horse in a manner that suits its age is bad for business.

Traditional breed demonstrations such as keuring and stallion tests show just how far the quality of the sport horse has come.

JUDGES

JUDGES

One of the most important roles in the structure of our current equestrian sport falls to the judges. This is because whichever horse and rider they award and declare as winner becomes a role model for all other riders—professionals as well as amateur and hobby riders. Their judgment determines what is considered good and correct in the equestrian sport. Pictures and videos of winning horses or winning rides at international levels in all countries reach thousands of people far beyond the actual show arena.

The majority of riders that spend their free time with their horses every day and train for competition look to these riders who win championships as role models, and emulate them. Ultimately, everybody wants to win, perhaps even become an Olympic gold medalist or winner of the World Cup. Judges represent the group with the most influence over the prevailing training system. They essentially decide how riding will be perceived, whether it is actually good riding, or not. For this reason, it's worthwhile taking a closer look at the qualifications and quality of the judges and their work, and at the quality of the judges' educators and their philosophies. Since I am most familiar with its system, I will use the German one as my example, but the same applies to other countries, as well.

Qualifications

The training and examination regulations of the German Equestrian Federation (APO) regulates in detail the comprehensive and lengthy education and qualification of the judges. In hardly any other country are the demands on a judge's competence as high as they are in Germany[2].

Most of the judges who face the exhausting task of judging shows on many weekends have invested a lot of time acquiring the necessary qualifications over many years with great dedication. They perform their duties with commitment and competence. However, in order to be able to meet the requirements of their task when judging demanding shows, they should not only be able to prove that they themselves have shown successfully, but also that they have comprehensive theoreti-

Top: A good tradition: experienced judges are commenting on a test. The rider learns from it, and the spectators understand what the judges are thinking and the reasoning behind the remarks.
Bottom: Friends at a show!

[2] see APO or *Handbuch Turniersport der FN* (see www.fn-handbuch.de)

cal knowledge at their disposal. In addition, they should have developed the necessary "horse sense." I believe that in order to be a competent judge one must not necessarily be able to ride successfully at Fourth Level, however, a judge should certainly have grasped the concept of the Training Scale[3], and know how it feels to sit on a horse that is loose and "lets through" the rider's aids—or, on the other hand, know how it feels to sit on a horse that is tense that is not letting the rider's aids through.

A competition should be the first test to see if the rider is following the fundamental training principles; if the horse being shown has been trained in a correct and natural way, or if its training has been forced. Let me quote an old rule: *The judges have to decide if the horse presents itself as a "leg mover" or a "back mover." The technical execution and correctness of the different movements should be of secondary importance to the judge[4].* (See quote by Erich Glahn, p. 31.)

A "leg mover," according to classical literature, is a horse whose head-neck axis is positioned higher—and with the neck made shorter—than its stage of training and muscle development allow for. This situation—when the horse's head carriage is created mainly by the rider's hands without involving the hindquarters—is known as "absolute elevation," and is described at length on p. 86. The expression "back mover" describes a horse where the thrust and energy created by the hindquarters can freely travel through the relaxed, working back toward the poll and subsequently to the mouth, causing the horse to be in a state of "relative elevation." This term refers to a correctly trained horse whose head carriage is directly related to the degree of collection the horse has attained in its training. For more on "relative elevation" see p. 85. Such a horse allows the rider to sit comfortably and relaxed, which in turn enables the horse to develop the potential of its natural gaits.

At a horse show, judges should not reward a trot that shows the biggest, most ground-covering strides or the one that's most spectacular without considering whether the horse is a "leg mover" or "back mover." In the normal course of training, showing highly expressive movements in the trot and canter with impulsion should only be done in higher level tests anyway, when the carrying power of the hind legs has been further developed.

[3] The Training Scale, to which the text repeatedly refers, consists of the following six elements in this order: Rhythm, Looseness, Contact, Impulsion, Straightness and Collection. See chapter 5, "Correct Physiological Training," p. 95

[4] to learn more, see for example, Glahn, Erich (1956)

Key Point: *In my opinion, when preparing judges for their task, it's particularly important to educate their "eyes" so they are able to judge the difference between movements that are natural and ones that are artificially forced.*

It appears that even our highest ranking judges lack the ability to differentiate between impulsion and tense, what I call "passagey" steps. A careful analysis by qualified individuals of the scores and comments at the 2006 World Equestrian Games shows this to be true. Horses that tensely "threw" their legs were rewarded with high scores in the extended trot. Horses with tightly held back muscles and disengaged hind legs were praised for their passage. I find this judging and scoring system to be questionable, misleading, and dangerous.

This may be a spectacular looking "showy" trot, but it is not without tension. Note that the right hind leg is far out behind the horse, his croup is high, and his tail held tensely.

A strong and independent network of experts in the field of judging would have a large influence on the quality of training, with its effect reaching all levels. Of course, the choice of judges and related oversight is an important responsibility of the federations overseeing dressage competition. There is a need for a panel to deal with disputed scores. However, the judges' decisions should not be contested by participating competitors, or by anyone with a financial investment in the results. This must be done by an objective committee.

Quality control and objectivity of judging should be an absolute priority. In the education of judges, classical principles must be highly stressed as the criteria for scoring. We must ensure that judges possess this knowledge for the benefit of our horses. In order to halt the current direction of competitive dressage and bring it back on track, dressage judges must be carefully selected and educated.

Of further concern is that the judging system in dressage competitions must be reformulated. The basis of the judging is defined (download the FN's *Ethical Principles* at www.fn-dokr.de[5]) but it must be logically and competently followed. There should be much more value placed on quality of training rather than the technical execution of the dressage test. Training methods that just create a showing "spectacle"—at the cost of the horse—should be rejected.

Independence

When making decisions, all judges should rely solely on technical criteria, freely and independently. Unfortunately, in equestrian sport today, this is not always the case. In fact, often it's the opposite: before a competition it's often the organizers of the show—or even the show's participants—who select the judges directly or indirectly. Under such circumstances, judges' decisions can hardly be neutral and objective. Currently, it's common practice among well-known riders to decide whether or not they participate in a certain show on the presence (or absence) of certain judges. Objectivity and independence, however, are indispensable prerequisites for honesty in the sport. The task of appointing judges to adjudicate at horse shows must be carried out by an overall governing institution, independent of the show's organizer and participating individuals. This could be achieved by lottery, for example.

The preliminary selection should be made using neutral and transparent criteria by the different associations, for example; on a national level by each country's dressage federation and at the international level by the FEI (Fédération Equestre Internationale). It should be made impossible for show organizers and participating riders to exert any influence on the composition of the judging team at any point during the selection process. This could be achieved by not announcing the names of the selected judges until before the day of the competition, for example.

Conversely, by proceeding in this manner one avoids the situation where a judge, having given an unpopular score, might not be invited again to a certain show. As said earlier, judges should be able to make decisions freely and independently.

QUOTE

Two excerpts from Erich Glahn's *Reitkunst am Scheideweg* ("equitation at the crossroads") published by Erich Hoffmann Verlag Heidenheim, pp. 89 and 93:

"The German equestrian Olympics commentator for many years, Dr. G. Rau, repeatedly criticized judges that ignored tense steps and insufficient activity in horses' backs. He had the sort of clear insight needed today, recognizing the source of the errors in performance; however, at the present time there is nobody like him pointing out judges' failings."

He continues:

"Identifying the *pure* gait, which means making the vital distinction between a 'leg mover' and a 'back mover,' is the first requirement. According to the spirit of a directive issued by the German Judges' Association, this should sort the 'wheat from the chaff.' Only after this requirement has been satisfied can further evaluation continue."

[5] See, for example, *Die Ethische Grundsätze des Pferdefreundes* ("Ethical Principles for the True Horseman") published by the FN

SPECTATORS

SPECTATORS

In our world's equestrian competition arenas it is not only the judges who play an important role, but the spectators, too. Many of the people who are involved with horses today no longer have their roots in agriculture, livestock farming, or related professions. Fundamental, basic knowledge of horses in general, such as their behavioral and physical characteristics, does not come naturally anymore. In fact, the opposite is the case: what in English terminology has become widely known as "horsemanship," meaning common horse sense, has become a rarity today. Spectators who have little understanding of the nature of horses or lack it altogether are more easily impressed by a performance that is based on the "over-expression" of a talented horse's spectacular gaits—not being able to see through to the underlying mechanisms at work. Not every judge is capable of remaining objective when being confronted with a crowd of exuberant spectators who express their enthusiasm for the performance in a noisy manner.

For this reason, it's important that the equine press educate riders and spectators and help them form opinions on a "broad" scale, and in particular be able to recognize when a horse is mistreated and assess gaits that may look dazzling but are produced "incorrectly."

Enthusiastic spectators watching the Three-Day Event at the 2006 World Championships in Aachen, Germany.

INSTRUCTORS AND TRAINERS

INSTRUCTORS AND TRAINERS

Instructors and trainers are most directly affected by what is considered "successful" in the sport of riding and showing. This group of professionals' remuneration directly depends on whether they win medals and ribbons–in the current system.

This causes conflict when it comes to the critical question of "how should I train my horse?" Success in shows is often linked to "economics" and sadly, not always to the training principles that have the horse's well-being in mind.

Initiatives such as "Pferde fair ausbilden" ("training horses fairly") launched by the German Association of Professional Trainers, demonstrate the presence of increased confidence in speaking out, which is a positive development. This initiative endorses the fact that the Classical Principles of riding are again being recognized as the basis for evaluating quality. It will enable us to see horses entering the show ring in the future, that at first sight, might perhaps appear less flashy, yet move in a more relaxed and loose manner. The benefits of proceeding in this way are valuable to every equestrian discipline.

However, there are also an increasing number of trainers with rather dubious theories and philosophies that they call "the principles of riding"—some of them even add the word "classical." Many of these "gurus" don't possess a solid knowledge of horses, including how to keep and train them appropriately. Here, it would be of great benefit if there were an institution that could inspect trainers' advertised services and—wherever necessary—debunk charlatans and "false prophets."

Top: The ultimate proud moment for every coach. Not every instructor is fortunate enough to have such a successful team of students. Chef d'Equipe Holger Schmezer with his gold-medal-winning German team at the European Championships in Moscow, 2005. Riders from the left to right: Ann Kathrin Lisenhoff, Heike Kemmer, Klaus Husenbeth, and Hubertus Schmidt.
Bottom: A young instructor doing her job.

RIDING ACCORDING TO CLASSICAL PRINCIPLES: WHAT DOES IT MEAN?

It is hard to find a way of riding or an individual "philosophy of riding" that doesn't consider itself to be "classical." The many interpretations of this term reveal how complex the topic is. One of the main causes for this lies in the fact that riders deal with a great variety of breeds as well as types of horses. A Warmblood, which has very big trot mechanics and a distinct moment of suspension, has to be evaluated quite differently from an Iberian horse, which naturally has less suspension at the trot and a "back line" that's considerably lower. However, there is a universal definition that does justice to all types of riding. A quote taken from the *HDV 12*—the riding manual of the German cavalry from 1912, which was also used as a basic reference for training horses by the world famous cavalry school in Hanover—serves as an example:

Richard L. Wätjen on Burgsdorff, a Trakehner, in an exemplary piaffe. Photo taken in Munich in 1936.

"The goal and basic principles of dressage riding are to train the horse so it can perform to the highest level of its potential, and to make it obedient. This goal can be achieved only when the horse is put into a 'position' or 'frame' that allows it to fully unfold its abilities, while preserving and furthering its natural talents. In such a correct position, the horse will be able to withstand the strains of service life for a long time[6]."

Here is what's crucial: at the center of this approach is the horse being allowed to develop into a strong and healthy athlete, which cannot happen with a mechanical and rigid training method. In my opinion, alternative training methods that carry the stamp of certain individual beliefs and philosophies might very well lead to success and be allowed to be called "classical," but only if they take into account the fundamental anatomical, physiological and psychological characteristics of the horse in general, and of the individual horse in particular. Famous respected trainers of the last century kept pointing out the importance of *time.*

Key Point: *Colonel Alois Podhajsky (1898–1973), former head of the Spanish Riding School in Vienna said: "'I've got time! I'd like to shout this out to every rider who suddenly runs into problems and can't come to an agreement with his or her horse. The phrase 'I've got time,' however, should also be remembered by every dressage rider, reminding him of the basic principle that we can achieve the highest goals in the art of riding only when we increase our demands on the horse in a systematic manner[7]."*

No athlete is able to perform to his utmost, peak at the right moment and remain healthy without having built up his body (and mind) over a significant period of time. It takes time to find the right horse to begin with, to discover its characteristics, special features, and get to know it. It takes time to gain experience as a rider so you can apply the correct aids. It takes time and a great deal of patience to train a horse until it's ready to compete while, at the same time, maintaining its physical and mental health—and to keep it fit until old age.

For this reason, the classical art of riding evolves over a long period of time for every horse and rider. Apart from possessing the necessary skills, "mastering" the art

[6] *HDV 12*, quoted after: Mossdorf, Carl Friedrich (1989), p. 52
[7] Podhajsky, Alois, ibid: Mossdorf, Carl Friedrich (1989), p. 142

A lengthening at the trot showing good impulsion; an appropriate lengthening of the horse's frame; and parallel diagonal pairs of legs. However, ideally, the horse's nose should be more in front of the vertical.

of riding also means any good rider must have a feel for the horse—his main concern being his horse's well-being. When a rider burdens a horse with his sometimes considerable weight, he should take into account the following, excerpted from *HDV 12*:

"The horse must learn to regain the body position it had when it was without a rider, and also move freely and easily under the rider's weight with a long and dropped neck. If it is able to retain this unrestrained way of moving, it relaxes. A sign of relaxation is when, at the trot, it moves forward while keeping the rhythm, covering ground without rushing, and striving to stretch its neck with its nose pointing forward and downward into the rider's sustaining hands. And other signs are when it has a springy swing in its back, carrying its tail naturally without any tension. Relaxation in the horse is the first prerequisite necessary for success in the entire course of dressage training[8]."

In the classical way of riding, the reins are only used as a sensitive aid to help the horse establish contact, not as an instrument of "navigation." Above all, the reins are definitely not used as a brake. A sign that a rider has achieved the highest level of refinement in the art of riding is the *"descente de main et des jambs,"* a principle that was first explained by Robichon de la Guérinière: it means the "dropping of hands and legs." If horse and rider are in harmony and have learned to communicate by using the most refined aids, the rider can even abandon his aids to a large extent, and let the horse finish the execution of the movement on its own—in perfect collection, keeping the same rhythm and impulsion. The classical art of riding understands "aids as aids," literally—and only as such: they help the horse to understand the rider's demands. Once the horse has understood them and responds to them, the rider can set them aside.

No matter if you study the works of Xenophon, a horse connoisseur and student of Socrates (about 400 B.C.), Robichon de la Guérinière (eighteenth century), or Felix Bürkner (Cavalry School, Berlin, early twentieth century)—the above-mentioned basic principles of dealing and working with horses have been valid across the centuries, until today. They are also valid for all types of riding—not just dressage, but for other, modern Olympic sports, and Western style, as well. The horse itself—with its potential and aptitude—determines the pace and way of its training, not the human being. One of the principles outlined in *Die Ethische Grundsätze des Pferdefreundes*, ("Ethical Principles for the True Horseman") published by the FN in 1995, explains it in the following way:

"Use of the horse for riding, carriage or vaulting must be adjusted to its aptitude and its ability and willingness to perform. Influencing a horse's ability to perform through the administration of drugs and actions that are not horse-friendly must be abolished, and perpetrators prosecuted[9]."

Sadly, these maxims are ignored all too often these days, especially in the training

8 *HDV 12*, quoted after Mossdorf, ibid: Mossdorf, Carl Friedrich (1989), p. 56
9 FN-guidelines, Bylaw 8 (www.fn-dokr.de)

of young horses. When the *HDV 12* was formulated at the beginning of the twentieth century, a young riding horse was destined to be a soldier's horse, which had to be built up systematically and allowed to develop over a long period of time, in order to produce an animal that was highly capable both physically as well as mentally. The decisive factor was to have a horse whose training was completed. The term "remonte" or "remount" was used in the classical art of riding and training of cavalry horses in the nineteenth and twentieth centuries and referred to young horses in training. A young remount was considered a horse in its first year of training, an old remount in its second, sometimes third year of training. This has changed in our time, very much to the disadvantage of young, not fully trained horses. An entire industry has been built up—not only around breeding and riding associations but also around breeding facilities themselves—that looks at the horse predominantly as a potentially very lucrative asset, as economic "material" or a "breeding investment."

Why training horses too quickly and incorrectly results in long-lasting damage–particularly in young horses—will be revealed in the following chapters.

BASIC EQUINE ANATOMY

The horse, the "unknown" creature

So far, I've introduced horse enthusiasts to the "functional anatomy of the horse" in more than 300 lectures. What keeps surprising me is how little background knowledge they possess to incorporate into their daily riding. Many training mistakes could be easily prevented if riders learned to recognize and respect a horse's physical and physiological make-up.

Every soccer or tennis coach has a relatively solid background knowledge of basic training physiology and its influence on the human body. In human sports, there is a huge advantage, of course, in that both trainer and student are humans, which enables them to reconstruct what impact certain training stimuli have on their bod-

"Foxtrott" has been trotting through the reception hall of the German Riding School in Warendorf for eight years. He is one of the most important teaching materials there.

ies, and what kind of feeling the different stimuli create in their bodies over subsequent days. When there's a horse and a rider, however, two creatures meet who both live in their own "universe" in every respect: human beings cannot know how it feels to be a horse.

A horse's sense of smell is keenly developed, almost as well as a dog's. Horses see movement more acutely than we do, yet have a completely different visual field, including a different perception of color. All their senses and reactionary systems are designed to survive on the steppe, within a herd, and to be able to recognize potential dangers in time to flee. To be able to persuade such a "strange" creature to cooperate with its rider and to participate in and master difficult challenges, not only calls for a rider's empathy, but also requires that he has a solid understanding of how entirely differently a horse experiences the world, and how different its nature is from a human. Only then will it become possible to ride a horse in such a way that it enjoys its work, and develops into a successful athlete without causing it harm.

Every rider should be aware that the minute he mounts a horse, he becomes a trainer, too, and plays a decisive role in how his horse turns out. Everyone, trainers and riders, must agree on the training goals: we want to produce horses that are relaxed, content and healthy, and who bring their riders joy in the dressage arena, or in other venues, as reliable pleasure horses.

Here is another matter I'd like to point out: regardless of how great a rider's affection is for his horse, or how "connected" he feels with it, a person should resist the temptation to anthropomorphize, and attribute human motivations and traits to it. Horses don't stand in their stalls contemplating ways their vices and bad behaviors could annoy their riders. A horse just reacts—directly or indirectly—to correctly, or incorrectly given aids, and to the experiences it has had with its rider or grooms. Resistance, tension and many physical problems often stem from incorrect handling. Training sessions and routines, demanding or monotonous, can lead to physical and mental imbalances. If the rider doesn't recognize the reasons but reacts to his horse's tension in a sharp and tight manner, he will quickly create a vicious cycle, which only he can eliminate later and with great difficulty. Riders must learn to recognize their horse's "signals and messages" and to interpret them correctly before this cycle can be broken.

A young rider who has decided "the head must be down." She needs to learn the classical principles for the sake of her horse!

"The head must be "down"!

This is a statement I hear far too often. Throughout the world on a daily basis, in training arenas you can witness how riders try to pull their horses' heads down in a position they think (erroneously) is "correct." When I ask these riders why they proceed in this manner, it often turns out that many of them—both amateurs and professionals—don't know why they're doing it. Sometime in their riding career they've learned that the head just "needs to be down." Unfortunately, incorrect ideas about riding are widely spread. The following chapters about equine anatomy and physiological characteristics will explain what's important for riders to know before training a horse. Once you understand the most important facts about anatomy and its function, you will know which types of riding are beneficial for the horse's health, which types cause damage, and why.

Before I begin, let me say this: the knowledge of the functional anatomy of the horse that you'll gain in the following pages has been tested and expanded in my practical experience over many years. To establish scientific proof by conducting large-scale research studies would be difficult if not impossible to achieve. I find it more important to explain the horse's anatomical and physiological characteristics in a way that's comprehensible so riders and trainers can apply this to their training methods.

In order to be able to understand the *functional* anatomy of the horse, you first need a basic understanding of its anatomy in general. Because this can be rather dry material, I'll try to make it as short, precise and comprehensive as possible. I hope you'll stay with me!

Why is an anatomy lesson worth your time—time you perhaps feel is better spent actually *riding* your horse? It is my feeling (and I touch upon this subject again in greater detail in the conclusion of this book) that in order to truly consider oneself a *rider*, one must be educated in the horse's basic physiology, conformation and behavior. If you know how the horse is built; how its skeletal, muscular and ligament systems work together; and also how its actions are controlled in part by instinct along with other aspects of the mind, then it only follows that you know better how to *ride* it.

Many of the incorrect training methods employed today are used in order to accomplish dressage "goals" that have become patently misunderstood through the years. For example, "hand-riding" or riding from "front to back" (see p. 86) is gener-

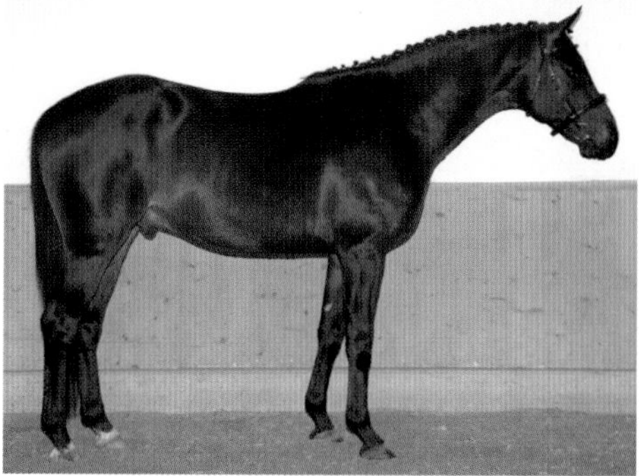

A young stallion at age two (left), and at age four (right). The horse's musculature will develop naturally with correct training according to Classical Principles (see chapter 5, "Correct Physiological Training").

ally used to force a specific head-set in a horse that is not adequately prepared for such a position. Another troublesome training method now known as "hyperflexion" (previously referred to as *Rollkur*—see p. 88) is used to get the horse to raise its back and "swing" it.

Both flexion at the poll and a horse that is working "through" its back are indeed aspects of dressage training that we all understand to be valid objectives. However, even a basic grasp of the horse's physiology would indicate that the position and length of the horse's neck directly affect the biomechanics of its back due to the extensive anatomical interconnections between the head-neck axis and the horse's trunk. Therefore, forcing the neck into an unnaturally shortened position, or placing the horse extremely round and deep inevitably leads to faults in movement and eventual degradation of musculoskeletal health. It is my hope that explaining these mechanics and the impact riding—both bad and good—has on them will help more individuals make educated, conscientious choices in the training of their horses.

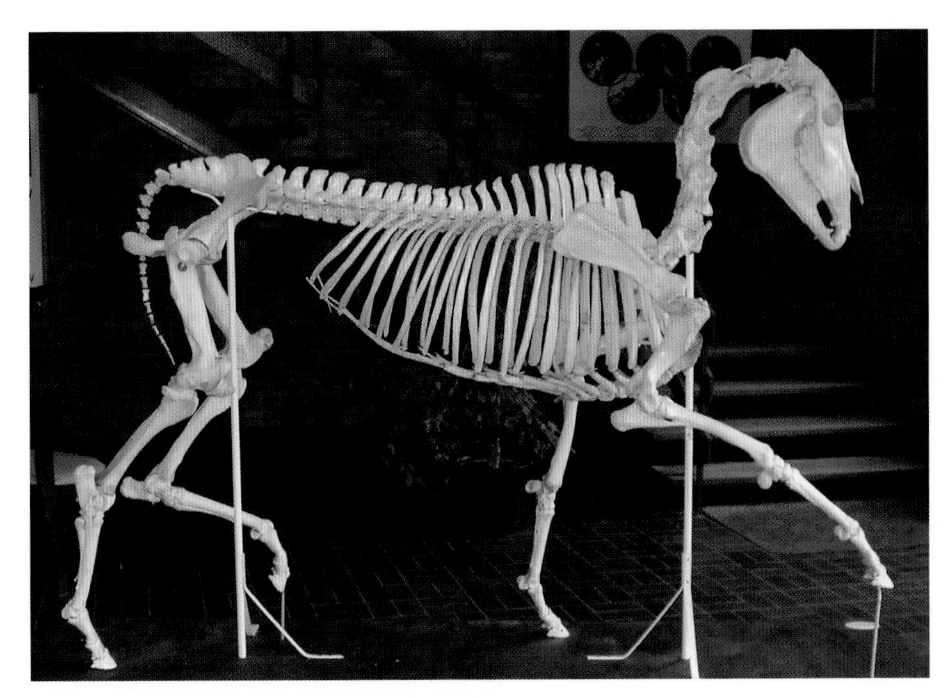

Foxtrott demonstrating correct footfall elevation at the trot.

The skeleton

Horses are large, heavy animals. Without the rider, a horse of about 16.3 hands (a Warmblood, for example) weighs about 1,300 pounds. This equals the weight of approximately eight men. For this reason, the horse's bones, ligaments, muscles and joints need to be well developed in order to carry not only its own weight but also the weight of the rider—and especially to carry him over jumps.

A big portion of the horse's weight is made up of the contents of the trunk and the abdominal cavity, which is "freely" suspended from the spine. Compare the construction of a horse's skeleton to that of a bridge: the front and hind limbs act like a pair of "support" pillars, and the thoracic and lumbar spines form the bridgeway itself.

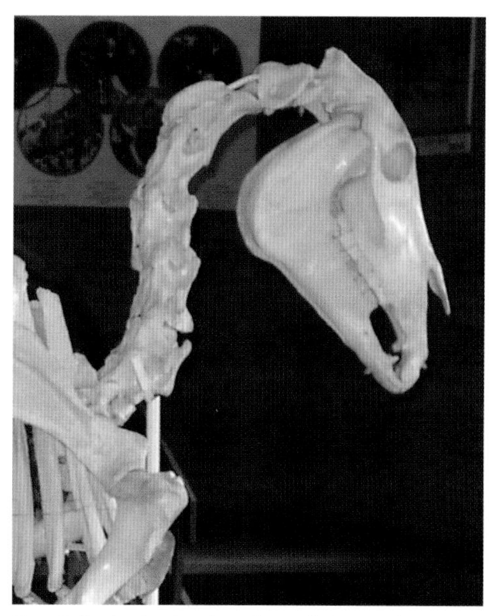
The skull clearly showing the poll (external occipital protuberance) at the highest point and the cervical spine beneath.

The *head* is attached to the cervical spine through a boney connection. The *external occipital protuberance* or *poll,* which lies above the *atlanto-occipital joint,* serves as the attachment site for the *nuchal ligament.* The skull accommodates the bit of the bridle in the area of the bars of the mouth. In this way, the head, with its dynamic motion controlled by the rider, has an important function as a lever that shortens or lengthens muscle and tendinous attachments along the cervical spine. The length of the head (and consequently its weight and position) plays an important role in this. *The temporomandibular joint* connects the upper jaw to the lower jaw. This joint can provide insight into the quality of the rein contact.

The *cervical spine*, made up of the *neck vertebrae*, consists of seven relatively large *vertebral bodies*. The way they are connected to each other dictates the degree of mobility of the neck. Forming an S-shaped curve, the cervical spine extends from the atlanto-occipital joint downward, and joins the *thoracic spine* about a hand's

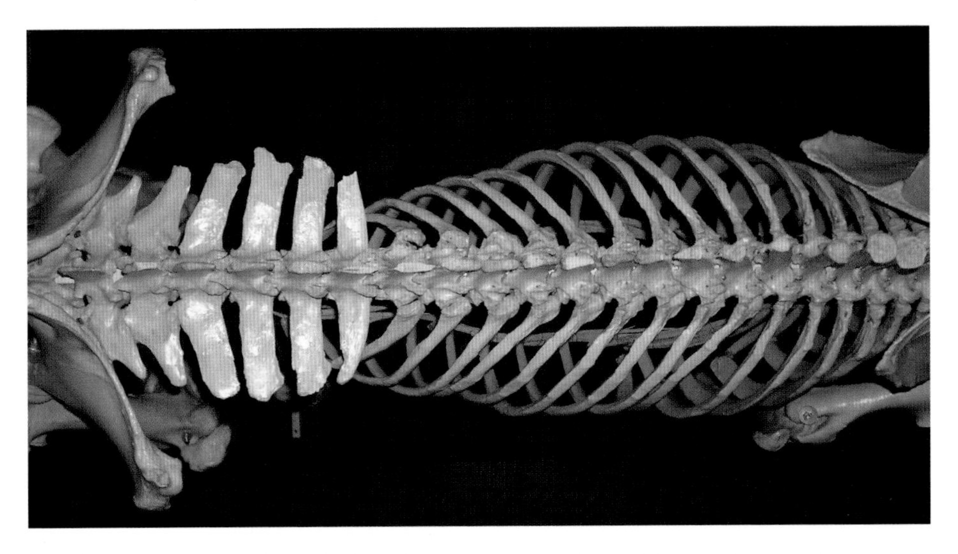

From right to left, the thoracic and lumbar spine as viewed from above. Note where the thoracic spine ends at the end of the ribs, and the lumbar spine begins, the transverse processes of the lumbar spine are rigid. *The saddle should never lie on the lumbar spine.*

width above the point of the shoulder between the shoulder blades. In horses that have not yet been "touched" by a rider, and ones that have been correctly trained, this section of the cervical spine runs in even, curved lines. If the clean "line" of vertebrae is "broken" between the second and third vertebrae (called a "broken neckline"), you can assume this is a sign of "hand-dominated" riding. (For more information about riding with a "broken neckline" see p. 92.)

The *thoracic spine,* which extends from the cervical spine to the last rib, consists of *18 thoracic vertebral bodies* that are considerably smaller and also less mobile than the vertebrae of the cervical spine.

These thoracic vertebral bodies are connected to the ribs below by small transverse (transverse means crosswise) processes. And above the vertebral bodies are protrusions known as *spinous processes.* The withers are formed by the extra height of the spinous processes that occur above the second to tenth thoracic vertebral bodies (these processes are significantly larger than the others). The first eight ribs are called the "true ribs" or supporting ribs. They articulate directly with the breast bone below, thereby providing the stable region of the rib cage, with the front limbs suspended on either side.

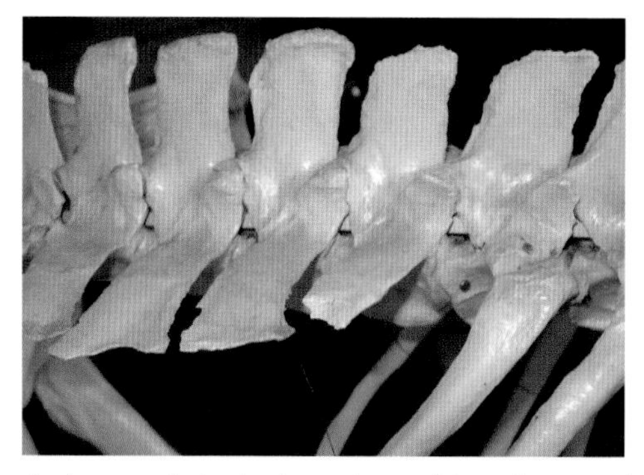

A close-up of the lumbar spine and its spinous and transverse processes (front of horse is on right).

The next 10 ribs, known as the "false ribs," connect to the breast bone by cartilage only, which allows the rib cage to expand with breathing. The portion of each rib that is closest to the spine is almost flat and parallel to the surface of the back, and serves as the bearing surface for the *long back muscle* (actually, a group of muscles), known as *longissimus dorsi* (for much more on this muscle, see p. 55). The individual thoracic vertebrae are firmly attached to each other by various boney and cartilaginous processes, which explain why this part of the spine is very rigid. Enormous stability is created by this construction, which is supported by the massive rib cage and corresponding muscles, adding further to stability of the thoracic spine[10].

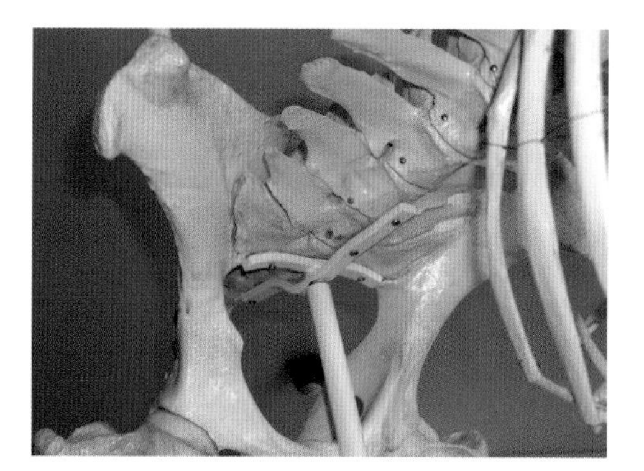

The sacroiliac joint viewed from the front and below.

The *lumbar spine* directly joins the thoracic spine and generally consists of six vertebral bodies, which are larger than those of the thoracic spine. (Most horses have six lumbar vertebrae, except Arabians, Przewalski's horses, asses, donkeys, mules, and occasionally other breeds of horses have only five.) Sticking out horizontally from the sides of these lumbar vertebral bodies are large, boney, immobile *transverse processes* up to 10 inches long. These processes provide attachment sites for the *longissimus* muscle and the *psoas musculature*. The absence of ribs makes this lumbar section of the spine more flexible than the thoracic spine region. On top of it, lies the strongest part of the *longissimus* muscle, which gives the lumbar spine a degree of stability that depends on the level of the horse's conditioning.

The lumbar spine then joins the *sacrum,* which consists of five *sacral vertebrae*

[10] In my opinion, we should seriously think about the current definition of "longitudinal bend" or "bend in the rib cage." What many people and riders perceive as bend in the rib cage (e.g. when riding on a circle), in my experience is based more on the condition of the muscles and the feel of the rider than on an actual bend of the thoracic spine. My hypothesis about there being very little flexibility in this portion of the spine is confirmed by the American researcher Dr. Nancy Nicholson (see *Cavallo* magazine, July 2006).

A relaxed, happy tail!

A horse holding his tail showing tension.

that are fused together. The *sacroiliac joint* connects the *pelvic girdle* through articulations with the *ilium* bones of the pelvis. The sacroiliac joint is relatively small yet, at the same time, is a very strong joint. The horse's entire pushing and carrying power coming from the hindquarters finds its way to the spine—and subsequently to the horse's trunk—via this joint. Its stability arises from powerful ligaments between the pelvic bones and the sacrum.

The sacrum joins to the *coccygeal* or *tail vertebrae*. These form the boney basis for the horse's tail and consist of 18 to 21 segments. In a moving horse, the tail serves as a balancing rod, and indicates the state of relaxation of the horse's back when being ridden (see photos above).

Along the entire thoracic and lumbar spine area, extending out from the center of each vertebra, are the spinous processes. As mentioned earlier, in the withers area, there are nine processes (from the second to tenth vertebral bodies) that surpass the other processes considerably in size. These long thoracic spinous processes form the shape of the withers and slope backward, whereas the ones attached between

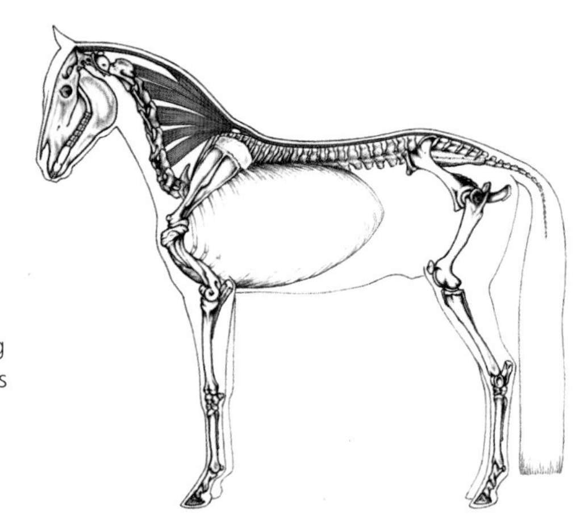

The "upper contraction system"–the ligament system of the cervical spine consists of the nuchal ligament starting at the poll and joining the supraspinous ligament at the withers area.

IN A NUTSHELL

For a horse to develop its *longissiumus* back muscles–the most powerful locomotive muscles in the horse's body–correctly, they need to work in a "relaxed" state and not in a shortened, cramped state.

- When the horse's head and neck are forward and downward, as in grazing, the relationship between the nuchal ligament and the supraspinous ligament serves to raise the back, releasing the *longissimus* muscle and allowing it to "swing" (see pp. 58-59, 72, 73, and 85).
- When the horse's head and neck are positioned too high, it tries to support the rider by tensing its *longissimus* muscle, resulting in a "hollow" back, resistance, poor gaits, and lameness (see p. 86).
- If the rider places the horse in an extremely deep and round position ("hyperflexion" or *Rollkur*), enormous tension is placed on the upper neck muscles and ligament system, and the back. While the horse's back does "rise," it is overstretched and tense, which restricts the hind limbs' ability to step under the trunk. The result is an uncomfortable, unhappy horse that is on the forehand with trailing hind legs, and unable to truly collect (see p. 88).
- Due to the complex interconnections between the skeletal, muscular, and ligament systems of the horse's neck and back, tension in one end of the spinal column spreads all the way to the other end. Therefore, the way the horse carries its tail vertebrae (which serve as a balancing rod) indicates the state–whether relaxed or tense–of the horse's back, which is in turn directly impacted by the horse's head-set and neck position (see pp. 51 and 84).

the lumbar vertebrae slope more forward (see photo on p. 49). The sixteenth thoracic vertebra—called the *anticlinal vertebra*—is the only vertebra that points straight up. The fact that these spinal processes incline in different directions creates an opposing force to the dominant muscle pull, allowing muscles to create tension to extend or collapse the back so that it works as a mobile and flexible unit.

This happens because of active forward-pulling forces created by the ligament system along the horse's topline (which shall be referred to as the "*upper contraction system*," p. 54); the respective muscles of the upper neck that extend into the back; the respective *opposing forces* created by the rear portion of the *supraspinous ligament* (extending from the withers to the sacrum—see p. 54); and the action of the respective croup muscles and muscles in the hindquarters.

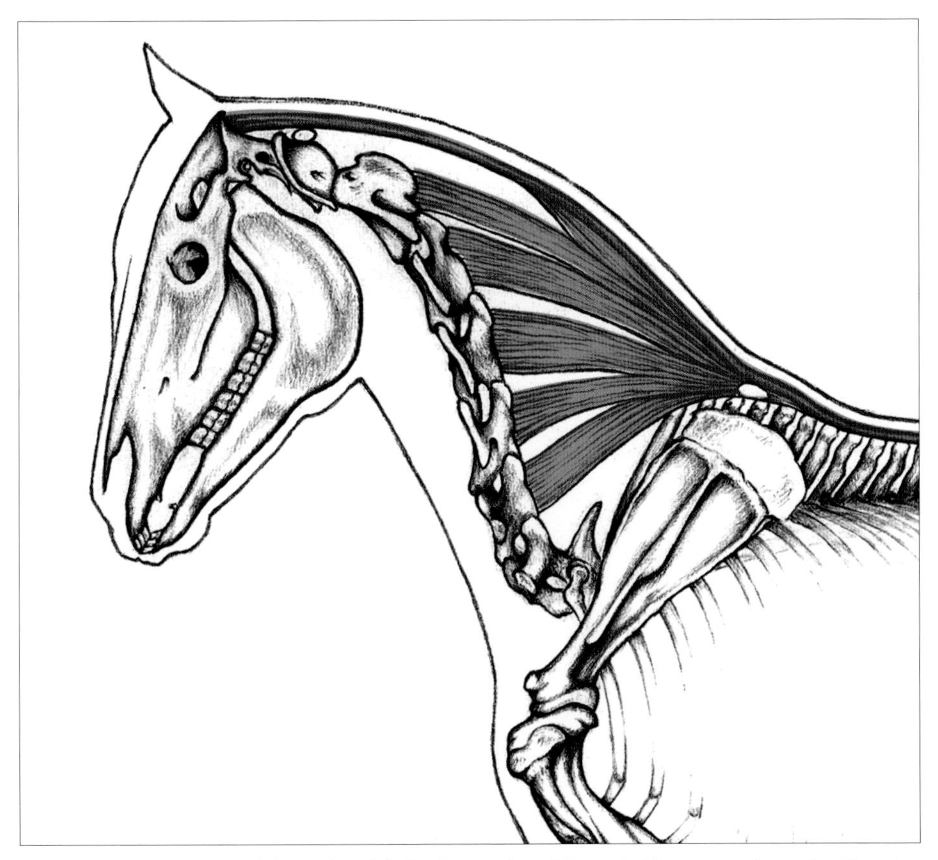

The nuchal ligament on top of the neck and the laminar portion of the nuchal ligament underneath, all in red.

The "upper contraction system"

The term "*upper contraction system*" refers to the ligament system of the cervical spine and back that runs along the top of the back, connecting and tightening all vertebrae from the poll to the sacrum. It consists of two main components–the *nuchal ligament* and the *supraspinous ligament.*

The nuchal ligament

The *nuchal ligament* is a powerful, elastic and fibrous cord that's about 1½ to 2 inches thick, and it follows the upper line of the neck. From the rear of the skull (at the external occipital protuberance) a cord (*funiculus nuchae*) creates the topmost line of the neck, extending to the spinous processes of the withers. It is attached, in the form of a broad "hood," to the sturdy tops of the long spinous processes of the withers. From this "hood," the nuchal ligament spreads as a fibrous, fan-shaped structure to the cervical vertebrae, C2 to C7. This portion of the nuchal ligament is called the "laminar portion" or *lamina nuchae*. It plays a decisive role in the functioning of the cord.

The supraspinous ligament

The *supraspinous ligament* (*ligamentum supraspinale*) runs from the hood of the nuchal ligament on top of the withers toward the tail. Because it adheres to the tips of the spinous processes of the rear thoracic spine and the lumbar spine, it connects these parts of the spine, finally ending at the sacrum.

The muscles

For sake of clarity, I'll categorize the horse's muscles into back muscles (the trunk), abdominal muscles ("*lower contraction system*"), neck muscles, and muscles of the croup and hindquarters. I'll mention the muscles of the front limbs only briefly.

The skeletal musculature is the active part of a horse's body. It is particularly relevant with regard to riding and training. These muscles are sensitive to correct (or incorrect) training stimuli. The skeletal musculature is also what makes a correctly trained horse appear aesthetically beautiful. The same can be observed in humans: every human being that exercises can see the impact certain training stimuli has on the body. And every beginner in any kind of sport is familiar with the consequences of his first attempts at engaging in new exercise: sore muscles! This painfully informs us of the existence of muscles we didn't even know we had. Our body takes note of our first riding lesson, especially in the two days following. Such soreness shows us that the body is dealing with the new training as the muscles start to adjust. A horse develops sore muscles just like we do; the only difference is that the horse cannot "talk" about it! Every experienced rider involved in training a young horse should keep this in mind and note attitudinal, behavioral, and locomotive changes in response. (See chapter 5, "Correct Physiological Training," p. 95.)

The long back muscle—*longissimus dorsi*

The *long back muscle* [*Musculus (M.) longissimus dorsi*] extends from the neck to the sacrum and ilium, is one of the most powerful muscles in the horse's body. It is for locomotion only; its purpose is *not for carrying the rider*[11].

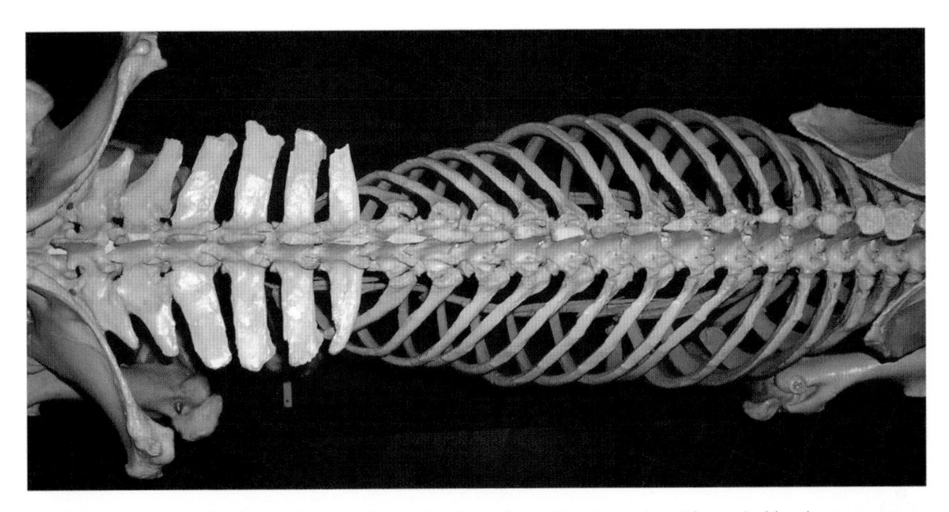

The *longissimus* long back muscle joins the entire thoracic and lumbar spine; it's carried by the transverse processes of the lumbar spine and the ribs (see drawing on p. 57).

Its physiological task arises from the fact that the *longissimus* muscle—this enormous muscle apportions itself into smaller and diverging portions so in effect it is a compilation of muscles rather than a single muscle) embeds itself between the spinous and transverse processes and the top portions of the ribs. This integration with

[11] for more information, see Bürger/Zietzschmann (2004), among others

The *longissimus* back muscle is one of the most powerful muscles in the horse's body designed for locomotion (not carrying weight). Before an obstacle, this muscle raises the front end of the trunk from its rear point of attachment—the pelvis.

When kicking out, the hindquarters are raised by the *longissimus* muscle's front portion (see drawing on p. 57).

the spine causes it to be a movement muscle rather than a postural muscle, which would possess a considerably greater amount of connective tissue and white muscle fibers. The *longissimus* muscles are fleshy with an extensive blood supply.

The *longissimus* muscle plays a key role in the training of a riding horse. Its rear base can be found in the area around the ilium, sacrum and the respective spinous processes (see drawing above). This establishes a functional connection to the pelvis and the sacrum. Its fibers run forward and downward toward the transverse processes in the area of the lumbar spine and the ribs in the area of the thoracic spine, as well as to various small boney protrusions of the lumbar and thoracic spine. The *longissimus* muscle extends along the entire lumbar and thoracic spine from back to front, ending at the seventh vertebra of the cervical spine. So, this muscle fills the entire space between the spinous and transverse processes of the lumbar spine, and the spinous processes and ribs of the thoracic spine. It extends along both sides of the spine, with its fibers running almost horizontally. It also covers numerous small muscles that connect the vertebral bodies. The following example explains its function:

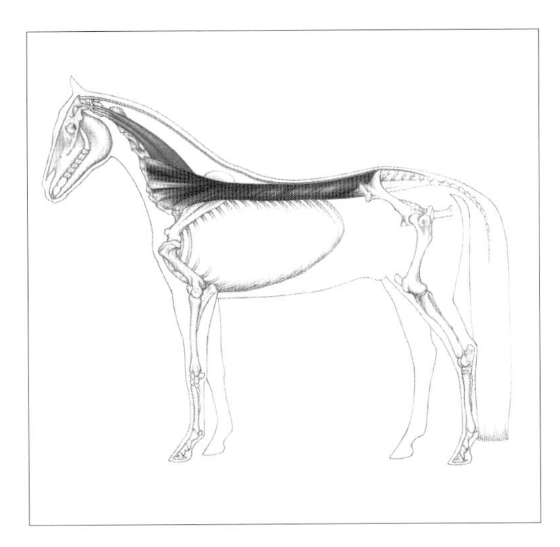

The *longissimus* back muscle (*musculus longissimus dorsi*) extends from the neck to the sacrum and ilium.

As a cantering horse touches the ground with its hind legs, it lifts its body from the ground and enters the phase of suspension. This raising of the trunk is achieved by contractions of the *longissimus* muscles on either side of the spine. When a horse jumps over an obstacle—or kicks out backward—this muscle acts in the same way, although in the latter, the forehand serves as a strut to raise the hind end.

The "still" back

Horses that trot or canter without tension, but also without true impulsion, exhibit a "still" back. They are easy to sit but they will never give their riders the wonderful

A medium canter with the *longissimus* back muscle alternately relaxing and contracting, allowing the back to move freely. However, the correct three-beat rhythm is not being shown.

In the levade, the *longissimus* back muscle has a similar function as when a horse jumps over a high obstacle. The duration of the lifting action in the levade makes the work of the *longissimus* back muscle more difficult.

feeling of being carried along on top of a wave that a truly "through" horse with a swinging back conveys. This type of horse usually finds it difficult to have a correct connection to the bit. When asked to stretch forward and downward, it does not raise its back muscles but falls onto the forehand because of its lack of impulsion.

This way of using the back is commonly found in horses that are trained according to the old teachings of Guérinière or the new school of the *Légèreté*. You can also see these horses in film documentaries of "masters" such as Nuno Oliveira. This type of training has no ill effect on the horse's health. It simply stems from a different interpretation of dressage than what is expounded in the *HDV 12*.

The swinging back

The swinging back is created with impulsion and this "pushing power" (see p. 108) flows through a relaxed back and is channeled through contact to the rider's hand. The six elements of the Training Scale can only be mastered when the horse's back is swinging.

The tense back

There are several types of tense backs. These include: horses that drop their backs (so-called "leg movers"), and horses ridden with an "overstretched" back due to hyperflexion (see p. 88). Tense back muscles are usually the result of a strong, backward-directed force on the reins. This tension blocks the movement of the hind legs and prevents impulsion from flowing over the back to the rider's hand. As a result, prob-

In the passage, the horse is required to combine forward-moving impulsion with a maximum level of upward "spring" or suspension. The high level of collection in the passage requires a large amount of strength in the hindquarters, which is channeled over the horse's swinging back to the rider's hand. In this picture, the forward-reaching hind leg is trailing.

Attempting to set the horse on its haunches by using severe rein aids makes the horse's back tense thus impeding the forward reach of the hind legs.

lems occur with connection and the rider's seat. The state of the horse's back muscles is a crucial factor; it alters how comfortable it is to sit the horse, its rideability, and very importantly, its health. Tense muscles lead sooner or later to leg and back injury. I am certain that a large percentage of cases in equine veterinary clinics are caused by tension induced by "hand riding."

The "lower contraction system"

The *abdominal muscles* function as the "*lower contraction system*," thereby stabilizing the trunk. Internal organs are suspended as in a hammock. When actively contracting, the abdominal muscles also lift the back. This, however, occurs only during the hind limb "push" and impulsion at the trot and canter. *The abdominal muscles do not actively participate in carrying the rider's weight.* Carrying capacity is often attributed to the abdominal muscles, but this only happens when the horse is standing still. When the horse is in motion, the abdominal muscles, along with the *longissimus* back muscle, are only used to create movement. One reason for this is that these muscles run across the abdomen in a curved fashion, which doesn't allow static muscle contraction. If they did contract in such a way, their attachment to the rib cage would collapse the thorax and impede the horse's breathing.

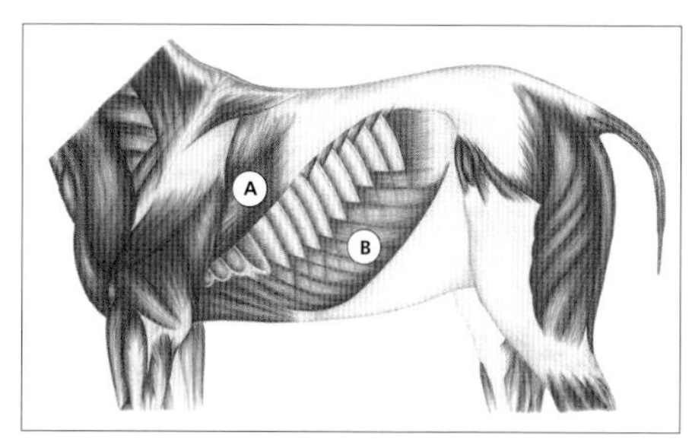

The musculature of the trunk with the (A) broad back muscle (*latissimus dorsi*), and the (B) external oblique abdominal muscle.

The "lower contraction system" is comprised of pairs of abdominal muscles: the *straight abdominal muscle*, the *internal oblique muscle* (oblique means slanting), the *external oblique muscle* and the *transverse abdominal muscle* (transverse means set crosswise).

- The *straight (rectus) abdominal muscles* from each side meet in the middle of the underbelly. There they interlace, creating the so-called *"linea alba"*—the "white line"—a tendinous band that connects the *sternum* with the pelvic floor of the pubic bone.

Extending along the flanks and the lateral abdominal wall are muscles of movement, which are characterized by an extensive blood supply:

The moment of suspension at the canter: The "lower contraction system" pulls the pelvis and the hind limbs forward under the center of gravity, and the horse's trunk compresses.

When the canter pirouette is executed correctly, the "lower contraction system" pulls the hind legs forward in rhythm.

- The *transverse abdominal muscle (M. transverses abdominis):* runs from top to bottom as a triangular, curved sheet of muscle—from the transverse processes of the lumbar spine to the lateral abdominal wall downward, into the *linea alba*. It serves to suspend the abdomen, and along with the other muscles, to flex the trunk laterally and to arch the back.
- The *internal oblique abdominal muscle (M. obliquus abdominis internus):* its muscle belly lies in the area of the iliac crest of the pubis, extending forward and down. It ends in the rear of the rib cage, thereby suspending it from the iliac crest. It also serves as suspension for the abdomen, and as a movement muscle for the hind limbs.
- The *external oblique abdominal muscle (M. obliquus abdominis externus):* its muscle belly occupies the side of the abdomen, overlying the ribs. Its fibers run downward and backward in a sheet between the abdomen and the pelvis. The strong abdominal ligament (*crus mediale*) runs downward toward the *linea alba,* thereby connecting to the spine of the pubis. The smaller pelvic ligament (*crus laterale*) extends toward the *inguinal ligament*, which lies in front of the pelvis and reinforces the deep fascia of trunk. It tilts the pelvis forward, allowing the hind legs to be brought under the horse's body.

A young horse with correctly developed upper neck muscles that produce a long convex-curved line.

To refute the widespread belief that the abdominal muscles carry the trunk and therefore the rider we can again use the example of the cantering horse. In the moment of suspension the horse brings its legs toward its body using the abdominal muscles, thereby raising the thoracic and lumbar spine to arch the back. The abdominal muscles actively pull the lower pelvis toward the rib cage, which raises the back. This phenomenon is difficult to observe externally. (It's less pronounced than in a greyhound, for example.)

The important upper neck muscles *M. seratus ventralis* (underneath and left) and *M. trapezius* (top and right).

In addition, the horse inhales during this phase, contracting additional muscles of the rib cage. This facilitates the forward pull of the pelvis through the hind legs because the ribs expand outward and forward. As soon as the horse enters the phase of support at the canter, the "lower contraction system"—at least its muscular portion—begins to relax: The horse's trunk opens up, the abdominal organs shift forward and the rib cage compresses to facilitate exhalation. During this phase, the rider's weight and the weight of the horse's thorax and abdomen create a downward force. If a horse's abdominal muscles did actively carry a rider, they would show active muscular contraction during this phase; however, this is not the case.

The neck muscles

If a horse is ridden correctly, the muscle system of the upper neck develops into a beautiful, long, convex-curved line. Apart from connecting the cervical spine with the shoulder, these muscles (most importantly the *M. splenius cervicis*) are responsible for raising the neck (see drawing on p. 65). When the head-neck axis is held in a low

The different layers of muscles, from deep (drawing 1) to superficial (drawing 4)

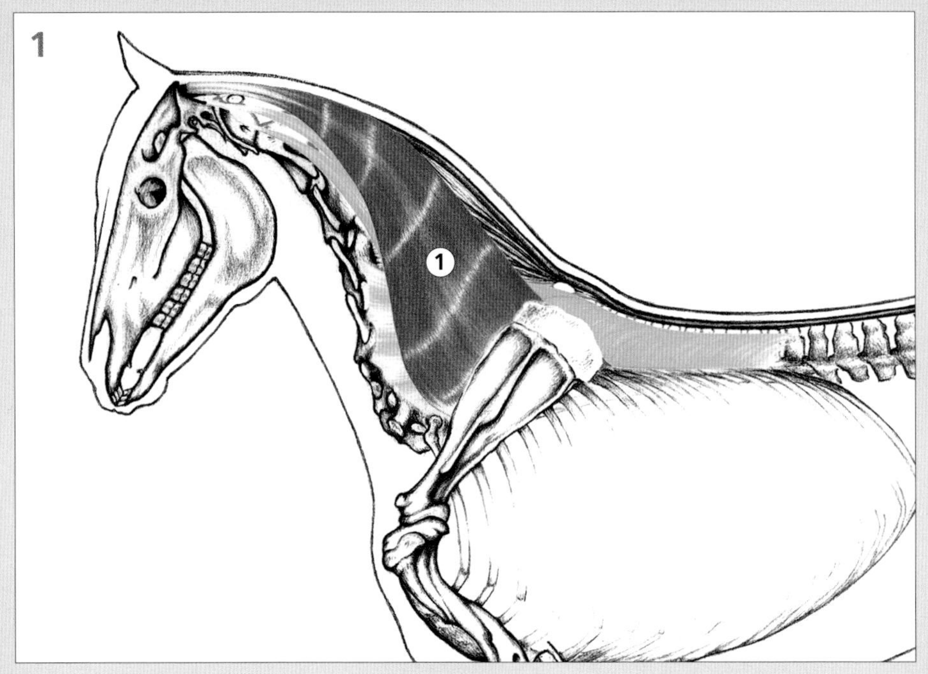

Musculus semispinalis capitis (1).

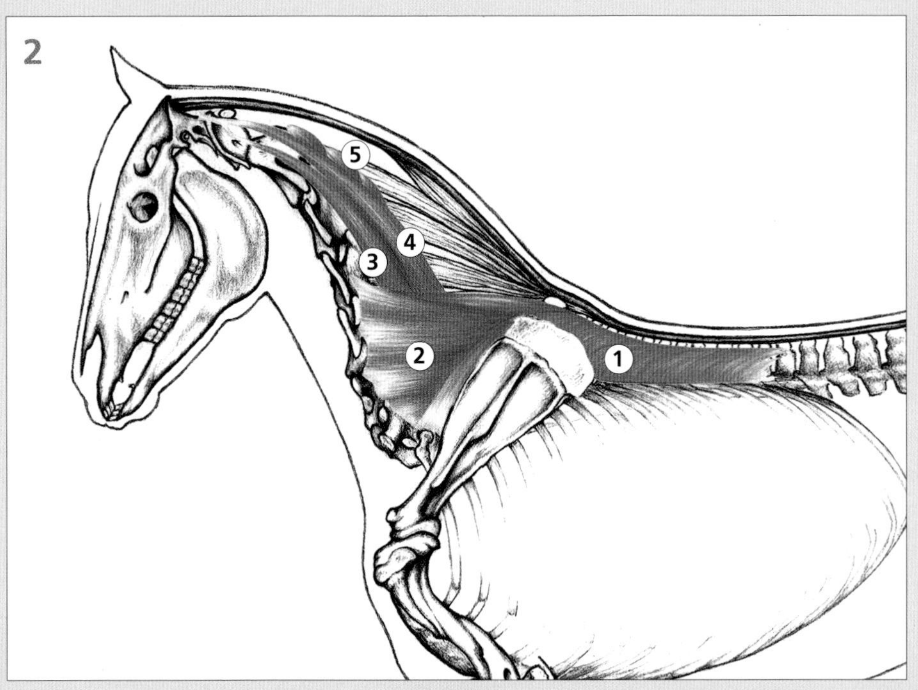

Musculus longissimus dorsi (1); *Musculus longissimus cervicis* (2); *Musculus longissimus atlantis* (3); *Musculus longissimus capitis* (4); *Musculus multifidus cervicis* (5).

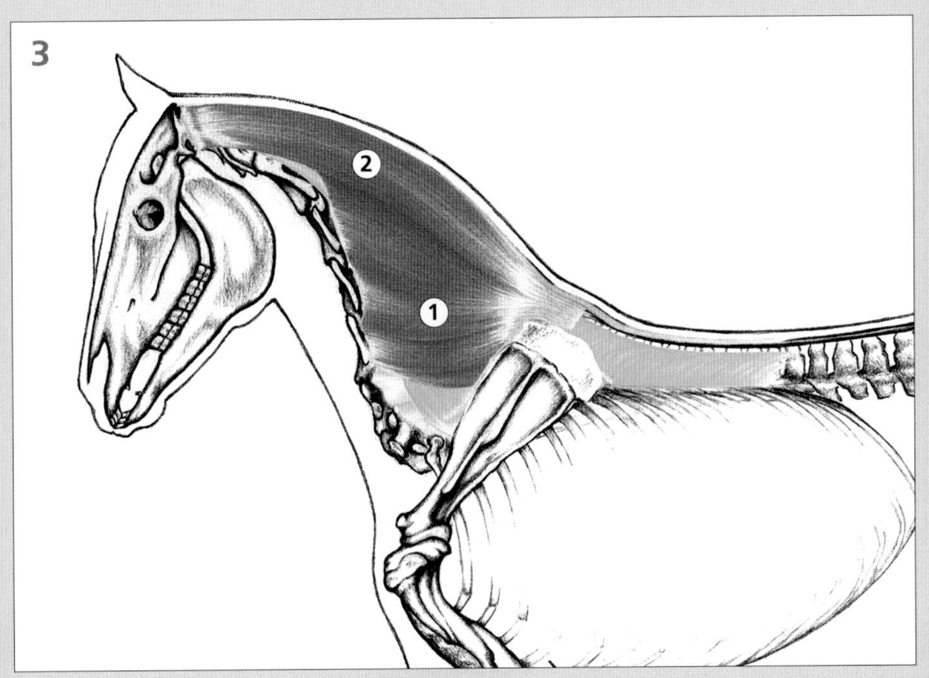

Musculus splinius cervicis (1); *Musculus splinius capitis* (2).

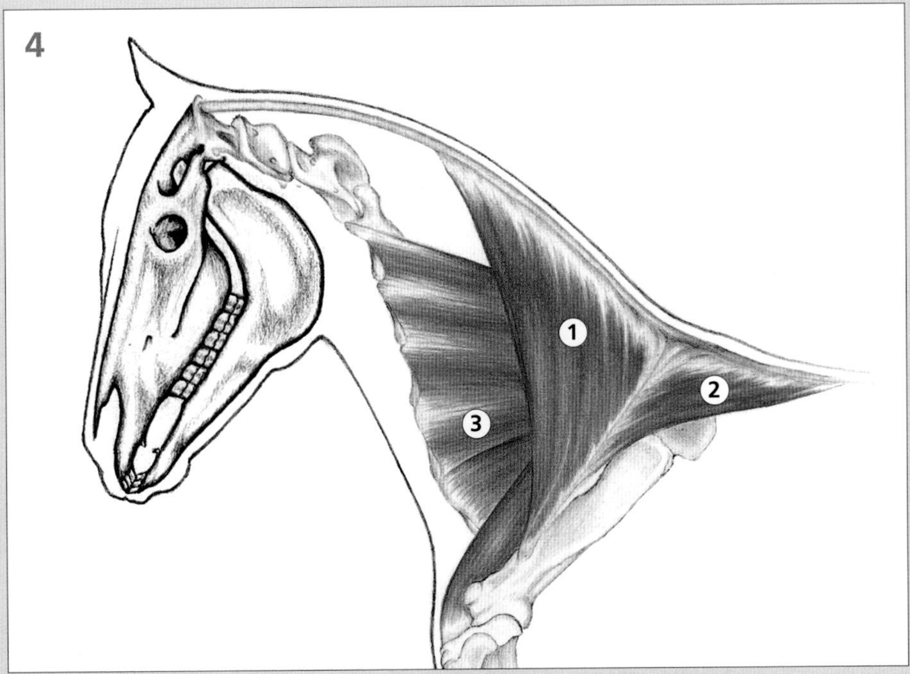

Musculus trapezius: Pars cervicalis (1); *Pars thoracica* (2); *Musculus seratus ventralis* (3).

position, the nuchal ligament supports the neck passively while the active muscles tend to direct the long spinous processes of the withers forward. This enables the back to be raised via the supraspinous ligament and thus releases the *longissimus* muscle. *The result is that these longissimus muscles are now free to work properly, allowing the back to "swing"!*

If properly developed, the muscle system of the upper neck is able to actively carry what has been accomplished passively by the nuchal ligament system, making it into an active system of the upper neck.

You can distinguish between long and short neck muscles depending on their location, as well as muscles that are classified according to their function (e.g. *rotator muscle, flexor muscle, extensor muscle*). A substantial portion of the neck musculature is located next to or above the cervical spine, with a smaller portion lying beneath it. The illustrations on pp. 64 and 65 show how these muscles are arranged around the *S-shaped cervical spine*. It also shows the muscular attachment of the neck to the front limbs.

The triangle that is formed by the rear of the cervical spine, the withers, and the shoulder blades accommodates a multi-layered muscle system that sandwiches the *laminar portion* of the nuchal ligament (*lamina nuchae*) in the center.

The most important muscles in this region (*M. semispinalis capitis, M. splenius cervicis* and *M. splenius capitis, M. spinalis thoracis* and *M. spinalis cervicis, M. trapezius, M. serratus*) connect the cervical spine to the ligamentous apparatus of the shoulder region, the spinous processes of the withers, the vertebrae of the thoracic spine and the inner sides of the shoulder blades.

This creates an extensive interconnection between the head-neck axis and the trunk, and it explains how the position and length of the horse's neck directly affects the biomechanics of its back.

The muscles of the lower neck

The muscles of the lower portion of the neck are located adjacent to and beneath the cervical spine as they spread through various single muscles between the skull and the cervical spine, between each vertebrae, and between the cervical spine and the trunk (sternum, ribs, and shoulder blades). These muscles lower the head and laterally flex the cervical spine. They also influence the lower jaw, the *larynx* (voice

An anatomically "ideal" neck for a riding horse with very good basic musculature.

A well-set neck of medium length, but the upper neck muscles are not yet developed.

box) and the *hyoid bones*. In a well-ridden horse they dwindle in size because they are barely active with correct training .

To say this another way, this means: if a horse's muscles on the underside of its neck are strongly developed, its training has been incorrect!

The muscles of the croup and hind limbs

1. Croup muscles

The *croup muscles* encompass the area between the pelvis/sacrum and the hip joint. Depending on their attachment site, they can serve either as flexors or as extensors of the hip joint.

The *extensor muscles* are considerably more developed. They are primarily responsible for the limbs' push off the ground. Later, when the horse is fully trained and lowers its haunches in collected gaits, they also perform the strenuous work of carrying both horse and rider.

The *flexor muscles* move the limbs forward in the phase of suspension and don't have to perform strenuous work.

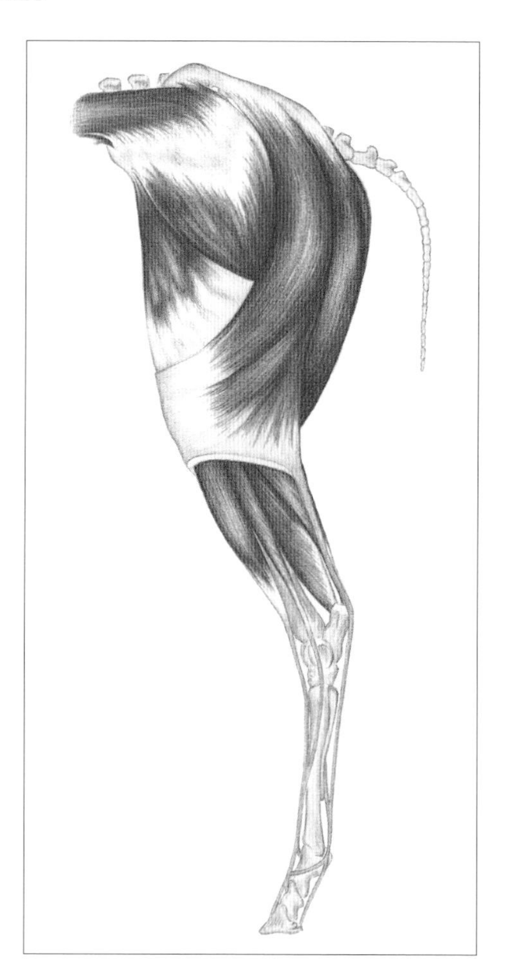

The croup muscles and hamstrings in red in hindquarter, and the *flexor digitorum longus* (toe flexor) and *extensor digitorum longus* (toe extensor) in red just above the hock.

2. Deep loin muscles

The *deep loin muscles* originate from the lower surface of the lumbar spine and extend toward the pelvis and the inner sides of the thigh. They assist in moving the rear limbs forward, bringing the pelvis forward as when cantering, and in raising the thoracic and lumbar spine. They're purely movement muscles, not postural muscles!

Like the *longissimus* back muscle, these muscles have no significant role in carrying the rider's weight. They also are fleshy muscles with a vast blood supply due to their physiological role as movement muscles.

3. Hamstrings

The *hamstrings* connect the rear end of the croup with the region around the stifle. They function as extensors of the stifle joint during the support phase. Through a parallelogram-type, tendinous connection of the stifle with the hock, they also serve as extensors for this joint. During contraction, the hamstrings work in unison with the big croup or buttock muscles. In the phase of pushing off the ground, these muscles are responsible for developing "pushing power" (see p. 105). In the suspension phase , they serve as flexors of the stifle joint.

4. Stifle extensors

The *extensors of the stifle joint* are located beneath the points of the hips in the front part of the thigh. They raise the patella and extend the stifle joint or move the limbs forward, depending on the degree of contraction of the muscles on the rear side of the limbs. When the horse moves with its haunches lowered in collection, the stifle extensors fix the patella in place and play a considerable role in the elastic springing action of the big joints of the hindquarters.

As fleshy muscles with a large blood supply, these movement muscles require extensive time to develop to be able to perform correct "flexion in the haunches," see p. 106.

FUNCTIONAL CONNECTIONS—AND THEIR IMPORTANCE IN CORRECT TRAINING

The passive ligament system of the trunk and the cervical spine

A horse can remain for hours stretched forward and downward with its mouth close to the ground; wild horses spend 17 to 19 hours each day looking for food. This position is a passive one, meaning the muscles are not actively contracting in work when the head is lowered to graze.

A grazing horse can carry the weight of its chest and viscera without any significant muscle effort simply by means of the "upper contraction system."

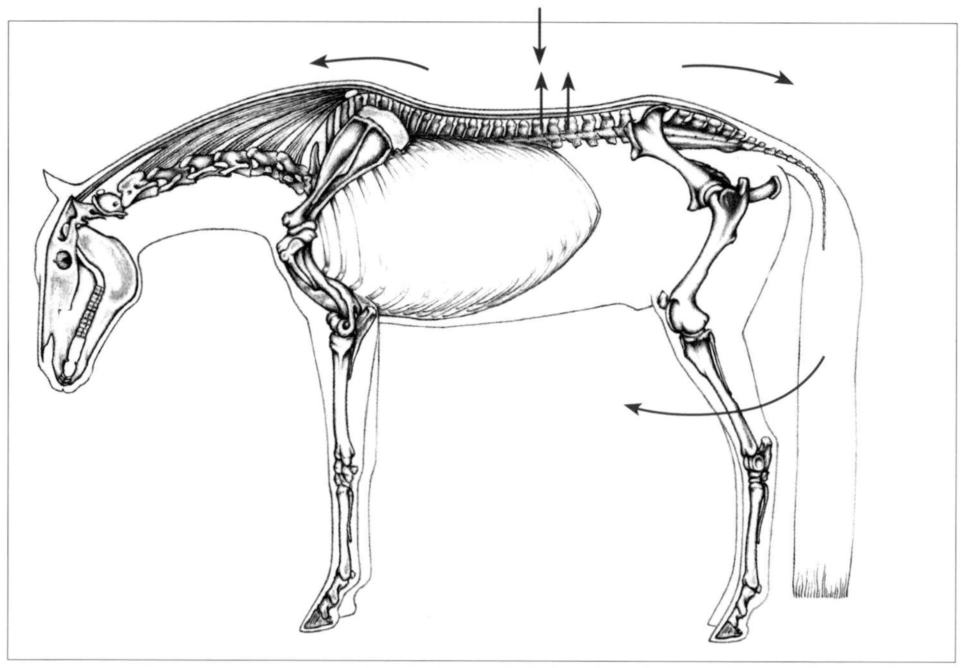

When stretched forward and downward, the upper neck line—via the nuchal ligament—raises the back into the desired position, which allows the *longissimus* back muscle to work in relaxation and remain free and actively engaged.

The effect of this posture on the spine

The cervical vertebrae's "S" form "opens up" when in this stretched position and almost forms a straight line. This means that the distance between the two attachment sites of the nuchal ligament—the rear of the skull and poll and at the withers on the tips of the long spinous processes—increases when the horse stretches forward and downward. Since the nuchal ligament is like a very strong, elastic cord, this exerts traction on these spinous processes. They are pulled forward, that is, raised *upward*, and this transfers force onto the supraspinous ligament, which subsequently raises the "bridge" created by the spine and muscles spanning the length of the back (see p. 54).

This enables a horse eating from the ground to carry the weight of its thoracic and abdominal cavity through the "upper contraction system" without exerting a large amount of muscular effort. This important physical insight is utilized in the classical art of riding by supporting the central rule to stretch a young horse forward and downward. However, riding forward and downward does *not* mean—and this is something that's often misunderstood—that the horse should run on its forehand. It only means that a young horse that has not yet developed the necessary muscles to carry a rider is given the chance to "carry" its back (including the thoracic-abdominal weight *and* the rider) by moving with a head-neck axis that is as stretched out and forward-down as possible, while maintaining a swinging, natural back.

IN A NUTSHELL

The loose, relaxed back is the decisive prerequisite for:

- A natural motion sequence in all three basic gaits
- Releasing the long back muscle (*longissimus* mucle)
- Allowing the rider to sit comfortably

This forward, or "light" seat, is the preferred seat to use during a young horse's basic training or when retraining horses; it is gentle on the horse's back.

Stretching forward and downward

A young horse that is ridden forward and downward correctly is able to carry the weight of its trunk and the additional rider's weight by the traction created through the "upper contraction system." This prevents misusing the *longissimus* muscle to support and carry the combined weights. A young ridden horse moving in this correct posture learns quickly to allow the "pushing power" of its hindquarters to flow through the back, over the poll into the rider's hand.

This is the only way to develop the indispensable connection from back to front (see chapter 5, "Correct Physiological Training").

However, this forward-and-downward stretched position not only exerts traction on the nuchal and supraspinous ligament system, but it also contracts muscles, especially those in the upper neck. *So, after working this way for 15 to 20 minutes, it's only logical to expect a young horse to want to raise its neck to avoid discomfort in the actively working upper neck muscles.* Old training principles account for this fact:

"If a young horse, after having moved with a low neck for 20 to 30 minutes, suddenly raises its head and neck, or tenses or collapses its back, this is not always caused by bad behavior. Rather, muscle fatigue elicits pain and discomfort in the neck. It serves no purpose to resort to forceful corrective measures or to attach side reins. Instead, you must stop the cause of the evasive behavior: dismount and hand walk the horse for five minutes. Soon after, the muscles will have recovered, and in most cases the difficulty eliminated[12]."

Today, unfortunately, riders often proceed differently when training. Many interpret the horse's desire to abandon this position as insubordinate resistance, and as a result, try to force the horse back into this position, using draw reins if necessary.

Key Point: *Such insensitive training methods often have disastrous effects on development of the muscles, relaxation of the back, naturalness of the movement, and health of the legs and the horse's mind.*

For people to be tolerant toward such training methods is, in my opinion, completely unfounded. The consequences of such training methods often become appar-

[12] Bürger/Zietzschmann (2004), p. 28

ent only after veterinary consultations about musculoskeletal or health issues become more frequent.

In the last few decades, modern horse breeding has produced horses with such good conformation and submissiveness and "readiness to suffer," that forceful training methods are frequently tolerated by the horse without major resistance. Only a few horses with obvious conformational faults that make it impossible to comply with a rider's demands, or horses with very strong character, oppose them.

Another mistake is to elevate a young horse's neck too early in its training, and to shorten (or skip altogether) the period of developing the muscles of the upper neck. Proper development takes one to two years. When the neck is carried in "absolute elevation," (the position created by the rider's hands, see p. 86) before it is ready, the nuchal ligament system is relaxed, but necessary supporting muscles in the neck are not yet developed sufficiently. So, the *longissimus* back muscle must assume the "carrying" work. But, this is only possible through an increase in the tonus in the *longissimus* muscle, which may increase so much as to cause spasms.

Optimal training of a young horse for a future career as a riding horse requires at least one-and-a-half to two years of building a foundation with solid, unspectacular gymnastic work. It may be helpful to remind you here that a young horse is at a fragile stage of its development. Only when its body reaches a level of physical "consolidation" should it be considered a riding horse. Then, it will be possible to further develop the foundation to incorporate "relative elevation," the correct head and neck position (see p. 85).

Why is it so important to have a loose back with supple muscles?

When looking at a horse with the skin removed, the first thing visible over the back is a broad, white, tendinous sheet, referred to as the *back fascia* (see drawing, p. 76). One function of the fascia is to provide mechanical protection, but its primary purpose is to bind together the *longissimus* and croup muscles, as well as the hamstring muscles. The *thoracolumbar fascia* also is the origin of the *broad back muscle (M. latissimus dorsi)*, which extends forward down toward the forearm. Through these fascial interconnections, individual muscle systems are bound together to form a functional unit. Consequently, states of tension are never restricted to a single muscle group. Usually, the most affected muscle is the *longissimus*, which is burdened

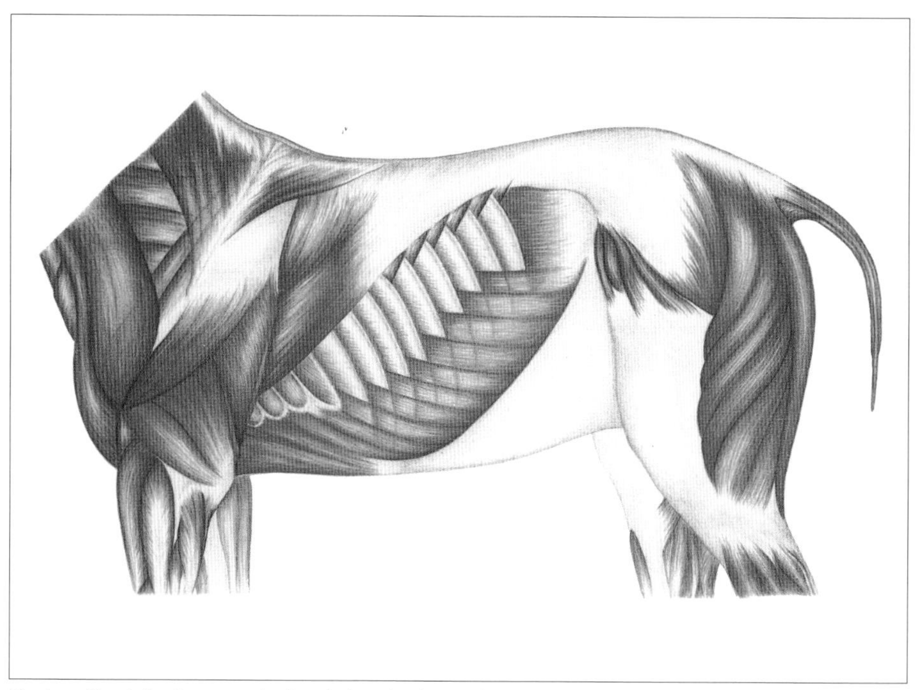

The broad back fascia covers the *longissimus* back muscle, and via the back connects the hind limbs and the forearm.

with about 130 to 220 pounds of weight oriented in a vertical direction. *Based on the anatomical interconnections mentioned, it is clear that relaxation of the longissimus muscle must be a rider's main focus. Tension in this muscle, rather than relaxation, directly affects the horse's rideability and all basic gaits.*

The horse's basic gaits

The *walk* is a striding gait, with a clear four-beat rhythm in eight phases. The bobbing down of the neck at every stride enables alternate relaxation of the two *longissimus* back muscle strands on each side of the spine. The working phase of each back muscle strand begins when the hind leg on the same side as the muscle touches the ground. The muscle strand on the other side, i.e. of the forward swinging hind limb, relaxes, provided the neck is permitted to work freely.

The most sensitive indicator of bad riding is in the walk. In order to perform an even, relaxed walk exhibiting a clear four-beat rhythm, a horse must be able to fully relax both sides of the *longissimus* back muscles alternately. When ridden, this is only possible if the head-neck axis is allowed to lower with each stride to place traction on to the supraspinous ligament. Lowering the head-neck axis results in a pull-and-upward lift of the spinous processes of the withers and a release of the *longissimus*, which is what you want to happen.

Key Point: *A horse that is forced by the rider's hands into an "artificial" higher head set than it is schooled for has to hold its longissimus back muscles in tension in order to carry the weight of the rider. This prevents the walk from flowing through the horse's body, and the result is an ambling, restricted gait and the four-beat rhythm disappears.*

The *trot* is a gait with a two-beat rhythm in four phases, and an airborne phase of suspension. If the *longissimus* back muscle is blocked, there is a delay and shorten-

Tension in the horse's body is immediately noticeable because the walk rhythm is disrupted. Here is a loose and relaxed, walk, although the rider's position is only satisfactory.

The walk is a gait without suspension, with a four-beat rhythm in eight phases. The horse's relaxation can be assessed by its tail. In this photo, the horse is showing clear signs of discontent.

ing of the forward-swinging phase of the respective hind leg; the swinging diagonal sequence of footfall (hind cannon bone and diagonal front cannon bone) is interrupted. Evaluating a horse's trot mechanics helps to identify a "leg mover" a horse whose head-neck axis is positioned higher and with the neck "hyperflexed" or flexed more than it's stage of training and muscle development allow for. Such a horse experiences excessive tension in the back (see bottom photo, p. 81).

The *canter* is a gait with a three-beat rhythm in six phases, and a phase of suspension. The three-beat rhythm is caused by the diagonal leg pair—inner hind leg and outside front leg—simultaneously touching the ground. These distinctive three-beats are maintained only when the *longissimus* back muscle "works" in a relaxed manner.

Again, a "leg mover" is unable to load the diagonal leg pairs at the same time and instead, canters in a four-beat rhythm. If horses are ridden in such a way for years, the effects are visible in the shape of certain muscles. These horses often develop a bulging and hardened *longissimus* back muscle in the area behind the saddle, which restricts their ability to perform a relaxed, rhythmically pure and ground-

The trot is a gait with suspension, in a two-beat rhythm with a diagonal sequence of footfalls. In this case, the right hind leg should step further under the horse's body.

The canter is a gait with suspension, with a three-beat rhythm in six phases. The three beats are caused by the diagonal leg pair (inner hind and outside front, for example) touching the ground at the same time. The longissimus muscle must be relaxed for this to happen. This horse is nicely uphill and stepping well under its body.

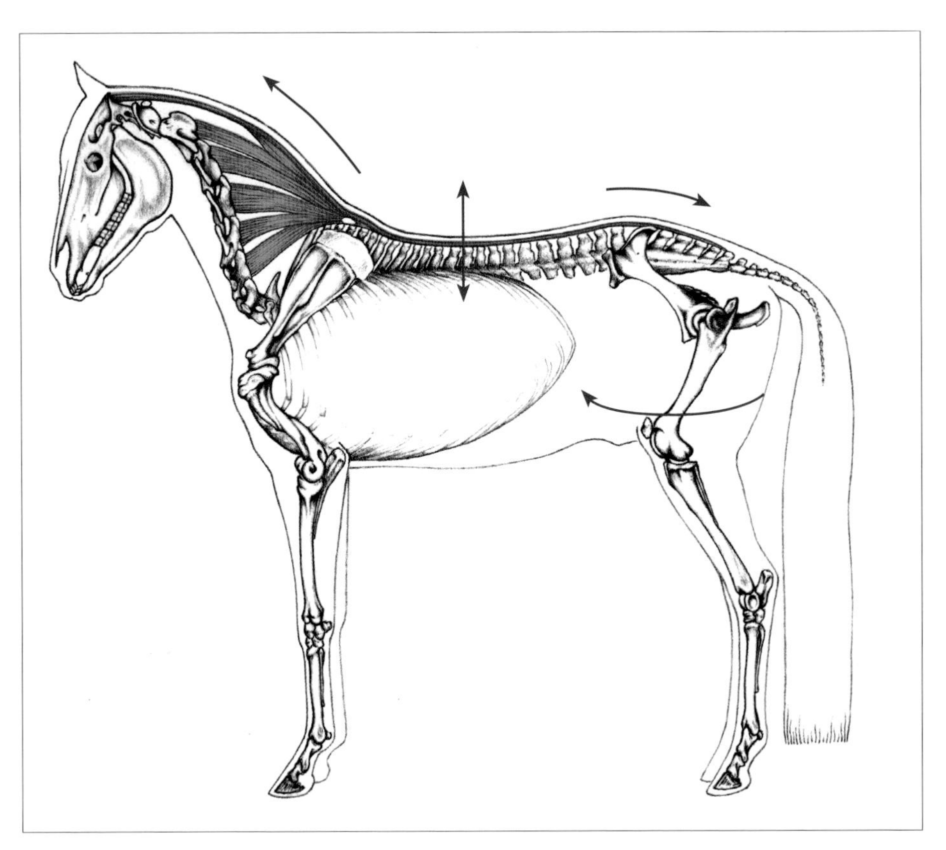

The nuchal and supraspinous ligament system plays a decisive role in the biomechanics of the back (see text on p. 72).

covering walk (see chapter 6, "Training from a Veterinary Point of View," p. 115).

In the book *The Rider Forms the Horse*, a benchmark of classical riding, Udo Bürger states the following:

"One sees horses win high level dressage tests, for example, responding to the rider's technically 'perfect' aids, yet the rider's seat is visibly bouncing on the horse's back at the extended gaits. Such a back is simply not relaxed; there is something forced in the horse's presentation; the harmony is missing[13]."

[13] Bürger/Zietzschmann (2004), p. 80

An example of exemplary trot mechanics, "flowing" through the horse's back.

A trot extension where the diagonal sequence of footfalls is clearly disrupted: the back is tense, the croup high, and the head-neck position is tight. This is an example of a so called "leg mover" performing a "show" trot—note the red lines indicating the height of the front and hind legs. To be correct these lines need to be parallel.

Sadly, such a picture is not uncommon: a rider using an "extended" dressage seat with very long stirrups sits on a young horse with an elevated neck and performs a fabulous, flashy looking trot.

What's happening here in terms of functional anatomy? In such a head-neck position obtained this way on a young horse, the nuchal ligament is not taut as it needs to be (see drawing, p. 80). The upper neck muscles are not yet ready to carry the back, therefore the *longissimus* muscle must counteract the rider's weight. The result: *the back becomes tense and loses its elastic swing.* The tension in the back muscles extends to the croup muscles and hamstrings via the afore-mentioned fascial connections (see p. 76). This causes a spectacular angling of the hind limbs, yet prevents them from reaching forward under the horse. Not only does the horse cover less ground, this deficit is also recognized by a lack of symmetry in the movement of

A rider with a good seat performs a trot extension. However, the diagonal sequence of footfalls is disrupted and the horse's right hind leg lacks reach. If the rider would allow the horse's neck to stretch forward about the width of a hand, this would reestablish a good diagonal sequence of footfalls, and the pair of raised legs would become parallel again.

the diagonal pair of forward-swinging legs (e.g. outside rear and inside front) along with an exaggerated action of the front legs, particularly in the extended trot (see photo, p. 82).

This body tension has even further consequences: tension also transfers to the broad back muscle (*latissimus dorsi*) and because the back has limited elasticity, the connection of this muscle to the horse's forearm causes restraint of this forearm. This results in the front limbs being "thrown" forward from the elbow with the points of shoulder unable to open up because the forearm is held so tightly.

Then, in order to make contact with the ground again, the limbs must be quickly pulled backward. When viewed from the side, the even "curve" of trotting hoof motion described by the legs in correct trot biomechanics disappears. As he moves, the horse suffers from increased impact and there is potential damage to its limbs.

Key Point: *Such a "showy" leg-throwing, toe-flicking trot, (which was called a "competition trot" in classical riding literature), causes a lot of wear on the horse's body, and is often the cause of leg injuries in the sport horse, especially in young horses doing dressage.*

QUOTE

> "When assessing horses for their degree of 'throughness,' such as in dressage shows, one should pay close attention to the purity of the gaits at the extended trot. This assessment should begin at an early level. The horse should exhibit a pure sequence of footfalls at the trot, just like at the walk. Basic mistakes at this stage should be given bad marks since they are fundamental and must be eliminated before you can proceed to higher levels. You cannot build a straight house on a lopsided foundation! Horses that have been prepared to exhibit excessive leg throwing (described above) at the trot will not be able to find relaxation in other gaits either. Often, they will not exhibit a free and long stride at the walk, and at the collected canter they'll be 'jammed' together, cantering with stiff hind legs. They'll lack the light and joyful reach for the bit because their necks are often too compressed, with tension and lack of suppleness in the poll, which, in turn, prevents the hind legs from swinging freely forward, causing uneven steps at the trot. Therefore, always bear in mind the following: if the horse takes uneven, hasty steps, do not react by applying restraining aids, but instead press and push the horse forward even more until you've achieved your objective: evenness, relaxation found through forwardness, and equal pushing efforts by the hind legs with increased action. Then the horse will no longer be excited and nervous during this work, and will do its best also at the extended gaits, flying over the ground freely and evenly[14]."

14 Stensbeck, Oscar M. (1935), 72-73

From the viewpoint of modern riding principles, such mechanics at the trot are not acceptable today, either. When a horse is "flicking" its toes with excess action, the sequence of footfalls of the *airborne* diagonal leg pair is disrupted. Often, the *front* legs leave the ground more quickly and are lifted forward and upward more than the *hind* legs. This destroys the purity of the gait at the trot. The sequences of footfalls at the walk and canter are affected in a similar way, with individual differences.

The head-neck axis

As discussed in the previous chapters, the position of the head-neck axis when viewed from the side has a considerable effect on the horse's back. During training today, one can basically observe three types of head-neck positioning—see below. To better explain the functional relationship between the head-neck axis and the range of locomotion in the horse's back, I call a "back mover" a horse with an "over-stretched" back, and a "leg mover" is one with a "hollow" back. And, when I refer to the *natural* positioning of the head and neck, I call it a "carried" back.

1. *Relative Elevation* or a "Carried" Back: the correct, *natural* head-neck position, reflected by the horse's age, type of horse, equestrian discipline and level of training. The Classical Principles of riding use the expression *relative elevation* with a "carried back" to describe this position.

2. *Absolute Elevation* or a "Hollow" Back: when the head and neck are positioned too high it is referred to as "absolute elevation" and is often coupled with a "hollow" back.

3. *Hyperflexion* or an "Overstretched" Back: the head and neck are positioned too deep. This has been called *Rollkur*, and, more recently, is referred to as "hyperflexion."

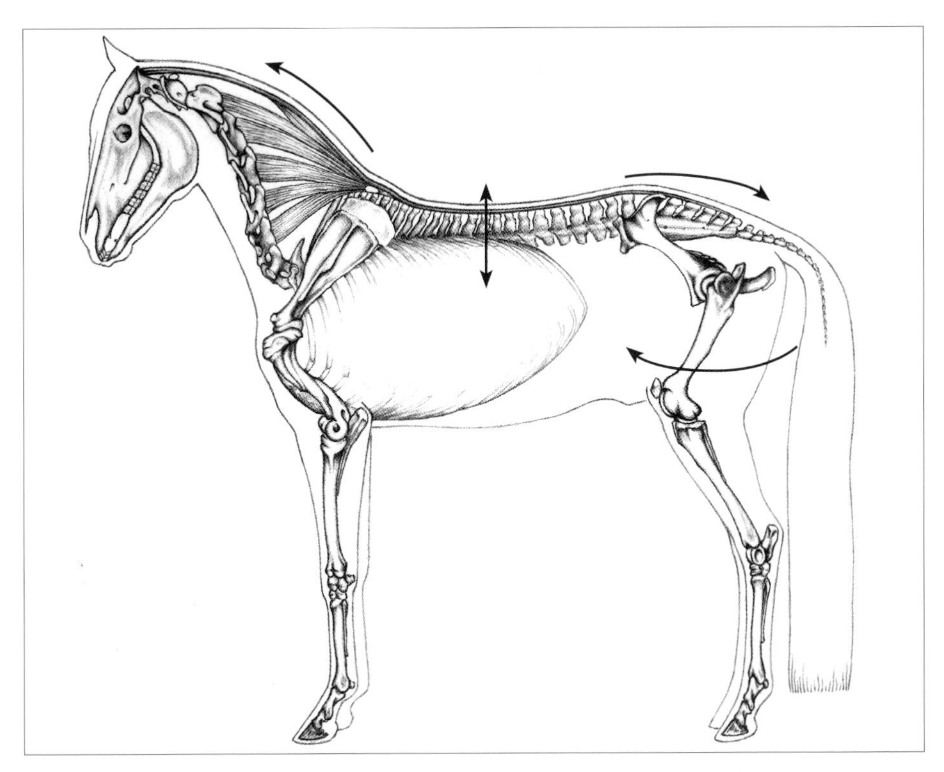

A horse like this in "relative elevation" with a released back allowing the muscles to work properly will be able to easily lower the croup and be able to step far forward under its body and the center of gravity (see arrows).

Relative elevation ("back mover")

Chapter 3, "Basic Equine Anatomy," p. 43, describes the anatomical formation of the upper neck muscles and their way of functioning. *"Relative elevation"* means that the horse's natural head-neck position adjusts and reflects the horse's progress and level of training, thus enabling these important upper neck muscles to work freely—without tension (see drawing above). In addition, this good position encourages strengthening and appropriate development of these neck muscles, especially during the first six months of a horse's training. As is generally known from common riding principles, one can expect muscle growth only if each work period is followed by a period of rest and regeneration. This natural head-neck position is dynamic, adjusts to the horse's gait, and is able to be maintained based on the age of the horse, its fitness, and the duration of each training session. The degree to which this natural head-neck position enables the horse to carry its back freely and without tension is determined by how skillfully the rider can influence his horse. The back's state of relaxation is mirrored by the purity of rhythm seen in the horse's gaits. A horse trained in this manner should be able by about its third year of training to develop the first beginnings of true collection (see "flexion in the haunches," p. 108). The expression "a carried back" means a back is working in relaxation, not a back that's flabby and "droopy."

Key Point: *Let me repeat for emphasis: the center of locomotion—that is, the horse's back—and its state of relaxation are the keys to success when training a horse—regardless of the equestrian discipline.*

Here is what I call a "passagey trot": the suspension is a result of tension in the horse's back. The hind legs trail far behind the horse, its tail is swishing, and the diagonal pairs of legs are not parallel. This gait cannot be considered a passage according to classical principles.

Absolute elevation ("leg mover")

A horse in "*absolute elevation*" is a horse whose head-neck axis is positioned higher and compressed beyond the level of the horse's training and muscular development (see drawing, p. 87). Consistently ridden like this, a horse will have difficulty supporting its rider. Initially, the horse tries to lift its trunk, which includes the additional weight of the

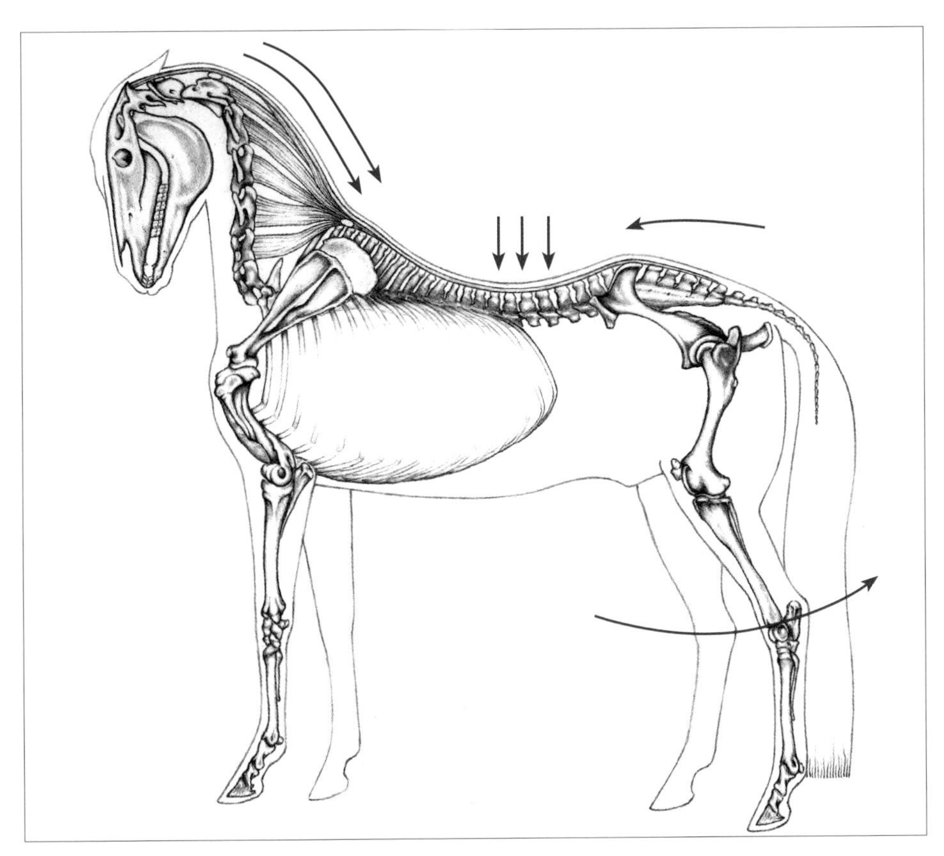

A horse in "absolute elevation" with a broken neckline, a neck that has been made short, a hollow back, with the hind legs strung out or trailing behind.

rider, by tensing its *longissimus* back muscle, but eventually has to drop its back, with the effect of losing the connection between its hindquarters and the rider's hands. The most obvious signs of this destructive method of training are unwillingness, tension, and resistance, with resulting poor basic gaits. Another sign is a rider having trouble sitting comfortably to the trot because of the tension in the horse's back.

Key Point: *To sum up: a horse ridden in "absolute elevation" loses the connection through its back, and is characterized by disharmonious gaits such as an ambling walk, a trot with considerable "throwing" of the front legs, and a canter that disintegrates to a four-beat gait with trailing hind legs.*

Especially at risk these days is the talented, young dressage horse—often naturally equipped with outstanding rideability—that curves his beautiful neck of his own accord making the inexperienced rider believe it is okay to "sit" on him even though he is only three years old. If, out of ignorance (or vanity), the rider just accepts this arched head-neck position and does not transform it into a real "stretching" position, he will sooner or later run into behavioral issues, "contact" problems, incorrect muscling, locomotion disturbances, or lameness. These contact problems and disobediences then frequently lead the rider to use various auxiliary reins, which not only fail to solve the original cause of the problem, but may aggravate it. After years, or sometimes only months, of moving with such a forced head set and accompanying tense back, the horse often develops mental problems and symptoms of physical wear and tear. In the worst cases, this renders the horse altogether useless as a riding horse. On the other hand, a horse that has been worked in relaxation and according to Classical Principles does not wear out—neither physically nor mentally.

Key Point: *One of the most common errors dressage riders make today when training is their tendency to favor hand-dominated riding—especially when working with young horses.*

Hyperflexion (moving wih a tense back)

The reason why riders are placing a horse's head-neck axis in an extremely round and deep position (well-known today as the *Rollkur* or "hyperflexed" position) is to get the horse to raise its back and "swing" it. But doing so with this method puts enormous tension on the upper neck muscles and ligament system, and the back via the supraspinous ligament. This does cause the back to rise but it is in an "overstretched" manner. Current research shows that horses moving with such a head-neck position demonstrate a very large amount of motion in their backs at the trot. It's dangerous to confuse this type of movement with the desired "swing" in the back just mentioned since an overstretched back is not relaxed during work. A great amount of movement in the back is not what is desired, but rather the relaxed way in which the back swings. Furthermore, an attentive observer will notice that horses worked regularly in this position have a straight, flat back line, with "inactive" trailing hind legs and no noticeable "flexion in the haunches" (see p. 108) during col-

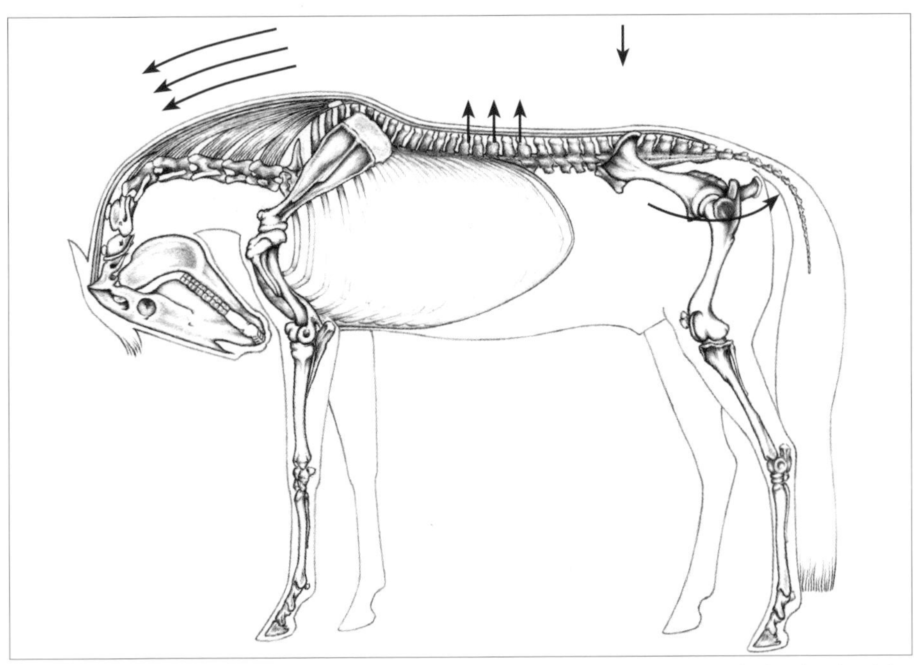

"Hyperflexion": a horse with an overstretched back. Due to the extremely deep position of the head and neck it is exhibiting a broken neckline, a strongly (incorrectly) lifted back, and a straight croup (overextended sacro-lumbar joint with the hind leg out behind).

lected or extended movements (see drawing on p. 89).

The trailing of the hind legs can be explained by the fact that the back fascia (see p. 76) connects with the large muscle groups of the hind limbs. This connection transfers any excessive tension in the back to the respective muscles in the hind limbs, thereby restricting their ability to swing sufficiently forward beneath the body during the suspension phase. The horse then ends up leaning on the forehand. In such horses, one can't discern the slightest "flexion in the haunches," neither during trot extensions nor in movements calling for the highest degree of collection. I've often actually watched horses that are not showing the slightest degree of true collection competing in the most difficult dressage tests!

A horse with a tense back and an excessively bent neck often tries to escape from the rider's weight by running away. This causes the rider to resort to even stronger hand influence, and into a rigid, "pushing" seat, often with the upper body inclined backward. To control this flight reflex, a horse that has been trained in this manner often needs to be tired out in the preparatory warm-up phase before a test. The same negative effects on the horse's health mentioned when dealing with horses trained in "absolute elevation" and with a hollow back also occur in horses that are trained with hyperflexion and an overstretched back.

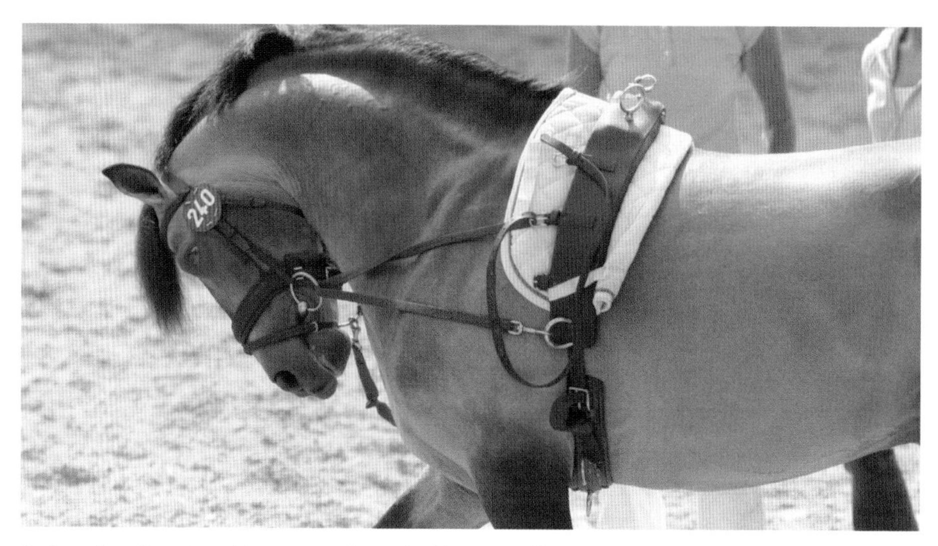

An "overflexed" neck position was used to train this pony stallion.

Even without the direct use of a rider's hand, it is possible to create tension in the horse's back through mechanical devices, thus ignoring classical principles.

Loose reins

Horses that are trained to work *without* contact may be seen to be "strung out" but have far fewer problems from the physiological perspective. Although these horses are relaxed (I'm thinking of horses trained according to the principles of Baucher, for example), such horses often lose the rhythm in the basic gaits and cannot develop impulsion. I personally don't object to such training methods because horses are not damaged as they are with "absolute elevation" and hyperflexion methods, but the fourth element of the German Training Scale—impulsion—cannot be achieved by proceeding this way. (For more on the Training Scale, see p. 96.) Also, in many instances, the horse's rhythm is not steady. According to Gustav Steinbrecht, in horses trained this way, the carrying power is well developed, but the "pushing" power is almost not developed at all[15]. Horses like this with "strung-out" movement often have a very strongly developed gluteus muscles, but weak extensors of the hind limbs and their abdominal muscles are often poorly developed—a sign of which is a big belly. However, such horses can generally execute all the movements requiring collection.

[15] Steinbrecht, Gustav (16th ed. 2004)

A "broken" neckline

Many riders are familiar with the sight of a horse on the bit where the upper neckline is "broken" at a point about two hand spans behind the poll: the upper neck line no longer runs in an even curve. Every experienced rider knows that this is undesirable—even bad—and is usually caused by excessive pulling on the reins. You may ask

This horse is showing signs of a broken neckline. Notice the area about two hand spans behind the poll (at the highest point in its neck). A broken neckline nearly always occurs at the neck's weakest point between the second and third vertebrae.

why it is that the neckline always "breaks" in the same spot. And why is it so difficult to eliminate this problem through training?

Chapter 3 introduced you to the muscle groups that are important in riding. You learned that the cervical spine is maintained in its curved S-form by the laminar portion of the neck (*lamina nuchae*) and the *M. splenius cervicis*, especially at the part nearest the withers. From other insights gained there (especially about the connection between head, neck and back) you can conclude that a neck lowered in relaxation opens up in a forward and downward direction, especially in the curved part of the cervical spine nearest the withers, thereby playing the key role in lifting the back through ligamentous and muscular apparatus.

In contrast, a horse whose back is stiff and tense cannot bring this curved section of the cervical spine into the desired stretch because the tense neck muscles and the tightly set ligament system literally hold this part of the cervical spine rigid. If the rider generates such a head set with strong hand influence, the neck is not able to bend appropriately, and the cervical spine "breaks" along its weakest part.

The occipital bone of the skull, as well as the first and the second neck vertebra are connected through a solid muscle system. The *M. rectus capitis* with its various parts and the *M. obliquus capitis* with its two parts connect these three boney structures strongly and firmly. As a consequence, the "broken neckline" occurs at the joint with the smallest resistance, between the second and third vertebra. You can eliminate this only if you can manage to loosen up and relax the *longissimus* back muscle and respective muscles of the upper neck. Only then can you create rhythmically pure "forwardness" in all three basic gaits.

A broken neckline is a sign that the horse suffers from hand-dominated riding. It can be less pronounced than seen in this picture. Due to the hard rein action, this horse is not in front of the rider's aids and does not have a natural, correct connection with the bit.

CORRECT PHYSIOLOGICAL TRAINING

It's not the purpose of this book to provide a complete training manual. At this point, I'd like to only mention the most important aspects.

The foundation for a horse's training is the Training Scale as formulated by the FN fifty years ago. It comprises six elements in this order: Rhythm, Looseness, Contact, Impulsion, Straightness and Collection.

A four-year-old showing good self-carriage, moving nicely forward. The neck is allowed to stretch and the tail is relaxed. The rider sits lightly to encourage freedom of the horse's back.

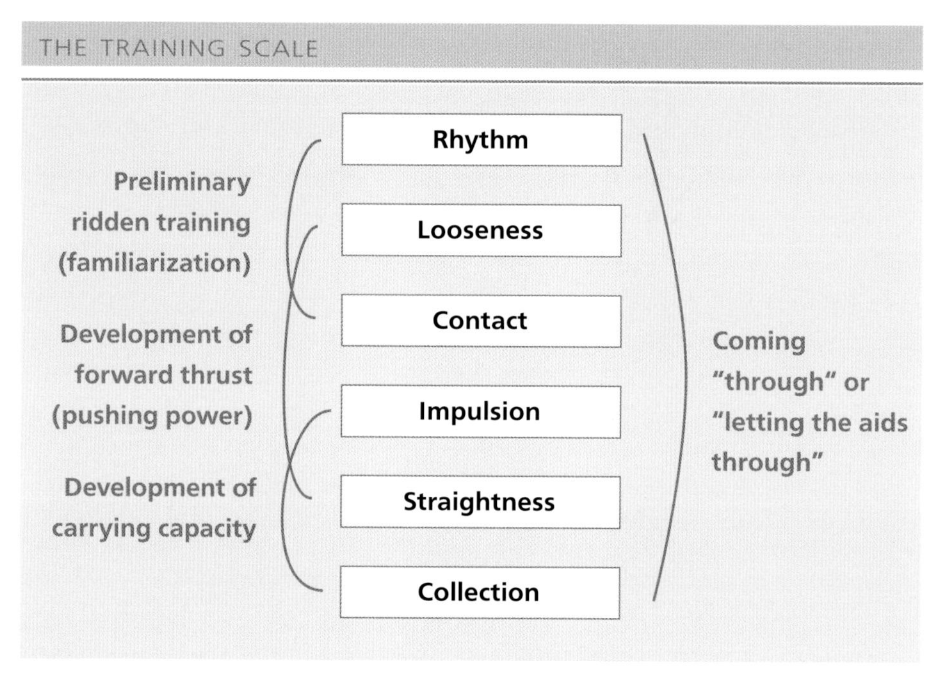

The training scale according to the *Principles of Riding and Driving* by the German National Equestrian Federation (FN).

The young horse

One thing is certain: the initial training stage should be basic and unspectacular. It should only serve the purpose of strengthening the skeletal muscles, developing forwardness and building a positive relationship between horse and human. Before a young horse is mounted for the first time, it should learn to stand still, be led with a relaxed attitude, and move in response to the handler's light signal. After this phase familiarizing the horse with ground manners and adding tack and equipment, work under saddle should begin by using the "light seat" (see photo on p. 73).

The first goal is for the young horse to be happily moving forward in rhythm. It should be allowed to carry its head and neck in a position that's as free as possible. The way this is accomplished is with soft, elastic, and even contact between the rider's hand and the horse's mouth.

As the foundation for work to follow, the first three elements of the Training Scale—rhythm, looseness and contact—should be achieved within the first one-and-a-half years, but it is inappropriate to adhere to a rigid time frame since many individual traits of the rider and the horse greatly influence development of the pair.

A young horse that tends to "curl" up, or run into the hand—a situation that causes the horse to wind up tightly—should be dealt with calmly and reassuredly. In the beginning stages of training, its back should remain as unburdened as possible, so, as mentioned above, ride such a sensitive horse at the trot and canter by using only the light and balanced seat. Care should also be taken to adequately stretch the young horse to eliminate tension in the *longissimus* back muscle. Running into the hand is extremely wrong and counterproductive, and if not fixed early on will interfere with future correct training.

In my opinion, even experienced trainers would benefit from reassessing the order and interdependence of the first two elements on the Training Scale. I believe, for example, that rhythm is impossible to achieve without a fundamental degree of looseness[16].

IN A NUTSHELL

When training young and retraining older horses, you can draw the following conclusions:

- The first years of training should emphasize calm and unspectacular work. These years influence the future development of the sport or pleasure horse.
- During the first two years of training, a trainer should focus mainly on the horse's mental relaxation and trust toward the human being as well as its systematic physical development.
- Practicing movements and tests is unimportant.
- The real goal lies in finding a relaxed balance while steadily increasing the horse's muscular fitness.
- Consolidation of the horse's rhythm at the three basic gaits, acceptance of the rider's correct aids and first degrees of "letting through" lead to the next phase in its development.

[16] Compare Schnitzer, Ulrich: "Grundsätze der Gymnastizierung des Pferdes," ("basics of gymnasticizing the riding horse"), 1996.

Lateral movements

The Classical Principles of riding recommend lateral movements as basic exercise. Many riders reject this as such exercises are thought to ruin the horse's joints. The opposite is the case!

To make a horse step forward and sideways is anatomically possible without any difficulty. Such movement also occurs in a horse's natural motion sequence.

Two half-passes to the left: The horse on the left shows good impulsion and swing as well as correct neck position. The rider has an independent seat and hand although her left shoulder could follow the direction of the movement better. The photo on the right shows tension in both horse and rider. The horse shows an over-shortened and broken neck line, and is leaning on the rider's hand. The rider is drawing up his knee and tensing his upper body rather than sitting with the horse's movement.

Key Point: *A horse that has been trained with correct gymnastic exercises and moves in a relaxed manner will not be harmed by including lateral work in its regimen. On the other hand, a tense horse can suffer musculoskeletal harm even when it is moving straight!*

IN A NUTSHELL

Benefits of leg-yield and lateral work:

- Familiarize the horse with the sideways-driving leg aid
- Improve suppleness and collection
- Relax back and neck muscles
- Fine-tune the horse to the leg aids
- Introduce the horse to collected movements: shoulder-in, travers, half-pass, renvers, canter pirouettes
- Set up communication between the sideways-driving leg and the diagonal leading rein (Note: not in travers)
- Supple the horse's stiff side
- Help straighten the hollow side as it improves the horse's contact with the outside rein

In all three gaits, lateral movements that require less angle have a collecting effect on the horse. These movements still require bend in the horse's body and an exact control over the horse's inside hind leg. A movement such as shoulder-in ridden with less angle—that is, on three tracks instead of four—encourages the horse to bring the hind legs further under its body and to accept more weight on them. The shoulder-in introduces the "carrying" function of the hind legs to young horses that have so far only developed "pushing power."

The half-pass is a beneficial lesson in preparing the horse to collect. Here you can see the horse's back is noticeably raised.

During haunches-in on three tracks, the outside hind leg follows in the same track as the inside foreleg. Since these legs form a diagonal pair in trot, haunches-in requires increased carrying capacity from the outside hind leg.

Leg-yield

In the first year of training, after the basics in rhythm, looseness and relaxation, and connection have been established, the horse can be introduced to forward-

This horse's flash and noseband are fastened too tightly.

This noseband is correctly fastened and the horse appears content.

sideways leg aids, and the leg-yield can be carefully developed. Working on this basic movement prepares the horse for later work in the lateral movements requiring collection. The leg-yield is also important in its own right since it serves to supple the horse's muscles.

How does leg-yield produce a suppling effect? Lateral movements on four tracks in which the forward-sideways hind leg steps behind the horse and rider's center of gravity create suppleness. The rider's inside leg drives the horse's inside hind leg forward and sideways under the horse's body. The horse's body is positioned at a 45-degree angle relative to the direction of travel.

The forward-sideways motion of the inside hind leg leads to an inward rotation of the femur. As the shaft of the femur moves forward and sideways under

Everything about the fit of this double bridle and the use of the reins is correct, however, the throatlatch is adjusted a little too tightly.

Here, the purpose of the double bridle is being misunderstood by the rider who is using the reins to force the horse into a certain head set.

the horse's body the tip of the femur (*greater trochanter*) that intersects with the hip joint (see photo, p. 105) moves in the opposite direction, namely backward and outward.

The outward movement of the *greater trochanter* causes a passive rotation of the croup muscle, which is attached there. This causes a pulling effect starting at the croup and going though the back fascia muscles and the *longissimus* muscle, which noticeably lifts the back. It is therefore extremely useful as a suppling exercise to incorporate leg-yielding into a horse's daily work routine. The saying, "The neck mirrors the hind legs" (Steinbrecht in *Gymnasium of the Horse*) applies well to this exercise. It is my opinion that riders should use leg-yielding, especially when ridden at a slow walk, as a frequent exercise. The movement is not used nearly as much as it should by today's riders. The positive impact of leg-yielding on resistances occurring in the poll, neck, and back also should not be discounted. Lateral movements such as shoulder-in, travers, and renvers have a similar effect; however, they

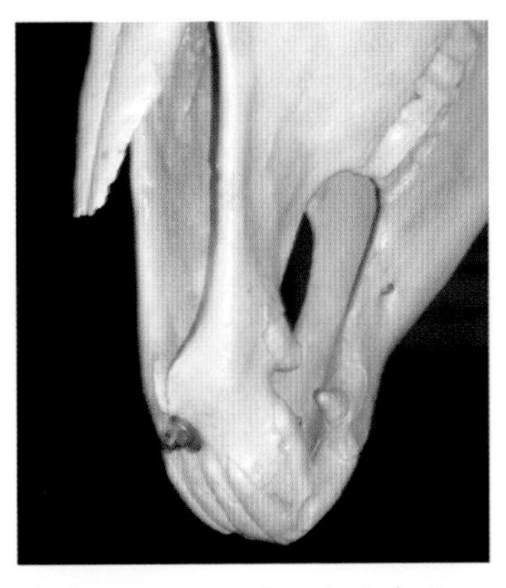

The bars are created by the branches of the lower jaw behind the two canine teeth. The width of the jaw and other characteristics determine, among other things, the choice of bit.

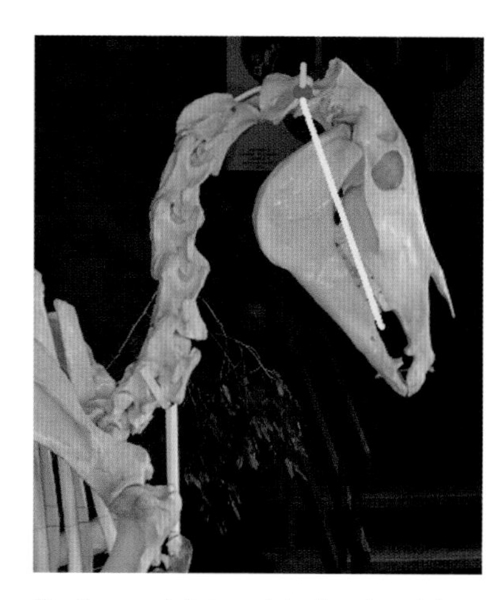
The boney skeleton of the head and the cervical spine showing the lever systems as described in the text.

have more of a collecting effect and less of a suppling effect than leg-yield.

Different opinions

According to their basic philosophies, the different schools of riding have differing approaches to lateral movements. The rider's seat in the shoulder-in marks a difference between the teachings of the *HDV 12* and the *École de Légèreté*. According to the *HDV 12* the rider sits so as to weight the inside seat bone and thus the inside "carrying" hind leg. When first beginning the shoulder-in with a horse, the still-developing carrying capacity of the inside hind leg must be accounted for by riding with less angle (for example, in shoulder-fore). Over time as the horse gains strength, the angle of travel can be increased, which in turn increases the collecting effect of the exercise.

In contrast, the French school advocates sitting in the direction of travel, in this case, to the outside. This seat makes it easier for a young horse to understand the sideways motion, but in my view, it omits the selective weighting of the inside hind leg. Horses that have been trained in accordance with these teachings show a high degree of flexibility. But the bending and lowering of the haunches required for collection, in the sense of that taught in the *HDV 12*, is not achieved through this training practice. In addition, it does not develop impulsion in the horse's trot or canter and can even cause impulsion to disappear.

It would be extremely rewarding if followers of these two training philosophies would exchange and combine their principles. Through a combination of the two schools, I see the possibility of achieving the goals set out by the Training Scale.

Contact

The quality of the connection between rider and horse determines the quality of the horse's training. The rider is connected with the horse through his seat, legs and hands—the latter represented by the reins. The term "contact" is often reduced to the connection of the hands holding the reins and the horse's mouth. The quality and refinement of this connection, however, is not only a result of a feeling hand. The way the rider influences the horse's back with his weight, and the way he applies his leg aids determine the degree of tension or looseness in the horse's entire skeletal musculature, and with it the suppleness of the neck, poll and the horse's back.

Key Point: *Contact in the classical sense becomes possible only if the horse lets its movements flow through its supple body, thereby eventually "seeking" the connection to the bit by itself. The bit is carried by the relaxed jaw muscles on the bars of the horse's mouth.*

It is crucial to note that this connection is not formed by tying the horse's mouth shut with a tight noseband. Correct contact can only be achieved with an active mouth; the mandibular joint must be able to move.

Key Points: *Nosebands of any type must not be adjusted too tightly, without exception. The jaw must remain mobile and breathing unimpeded; otherwise, tension will build that transfers to the entire body. Riding with hands that are too hard, and continuously influencing the horse with overly strong rein aids have a negative effect on the horse's entire body.*

In my opinion, you should try to use a soft, well-fitted snaffle bit (single- or double-jointed) during a horse's entire course of training. The anatomy of the lower jaw, unique to each horse, determines the choice of the bit.

The purpose of using a sharper bit should only be to *refine* the aids. It should never become a means of coercion to control the horse or to force it into a certain head set.

To help you understand the physiological effects of pulling the head and neck back in a "backward-acting" rein aid, I'd like to briefly address the boney anatomy of the head-neck connection.

In a live horse, the area around the throatlatch appears to be a robust, massive connection between the head and the neck. When looking at a skeleton, however, you can see that the only boney connection of the skull to the cervical spine is located quite high up with the rest of the head and neck, including the first few neck vertebrae, only connected through soft tissue parts (see photo, p. 102).

The atlanto-occipital joint is a small joint, which primarily allows for vertical movement (nodding-type movement); lateral flexion is possible to a small degree only. This is caused, in part, by the way the joint is constructed, and partly by the boney processes that restrict lateral flexion. This is one reason why a horse can flex laterally only slightly—as the Classical Principles of riding claim.

The boney anatomy of this area also explains why a backward-acting rein creates such a big lever action: viewed from the side, the poll can be considered a pivot point for the skull. If a horse wants to lift its head—i.e. stretch its poll—while its neck remains fixed, there has to be a muscle pull on the occipital bone (see photo, in red). This action is executed by the muscles *Mm. recti capitis dorsales* (major and minor), the *M. semispinalis capitis* as well as the *M. splenius capitis*. Their "lever arms" are very short (about 1.6 to 2.4 inches, see green line in photo). The length of the lever that the rider has available for his rein influence extends from the poll to the bars of the mouth (see yellow line in photo). A pull on the reins in order to bend the neck acts on the bars of the mouth. The connecting line between poll and bars is between 11.8 to 15.7 inches (depending on the length of the horse's head). This creates a lever ratio of approximately 1:7 to 1:10.

To simplify matters, calculating with 1:10 yields 66 pounds of force (lbf) on each rein, which creates a pull of 132 lbf on each bar of the mouth. *If the mouth of the horse doesn't yield to this pressure, a force of up to 1,323 lbf occurs at the occipital bone–approximately 10 times the amount acting on the bars!* Now, how can a horse's back swing if it has been fixed by hundreds of pounds of pulling action via the back's ligament and muscle system, as explained to you earlier? How can this horse possibly allow its rider to sit comfortably with such tension? And, how can its back—and legs—remain healthy?

Key Point: *For this reason, the Classical Principles of riding a horse from back to front, toward the rider's hand, is a vital one if you want to maintain a healthy and sound riding horse! The correct set of the head and neck, which depends on the horse's age and experience (known as "relative elevation," p. 85) is* *achieved automatically with correct contact. The opposite system—riding a horse from front to back—inevitably leads to faults in movement and impairs the horse's musculoskeletal health. A good rider must use his aids like a sharp knife—cautiously and gingerly!*

Unfortunately, we often see an older and more experienced rider, maybe with heavier body weight, able to powerfully influence a horse. This leads to enormous damage as this rider—unknowingly—pulls the horse together with overbearing aids. Riders like this are frequently prone to demanding unconditional obedience from the horse. They ignore important signals the horse is expressing, for example, that resistance to the aids is related to muscle pain.

For such riders, it is easy to for them to physically force even a very young horse with a tense back—that is not ready—to perform piaffe and passage, which sadly still raises cheers and receives high scores in competition.

I'd like to emphasize that every attempt to mechanically put the horse's head and neck into a specific set frame using one's hands is the beginning of the end, and has far-reaching training consequences.

Using draw reins

Draw reins multiply the force effect the bit has on the bars, and fundamentally act to pull the head and neck in a backward direction (see photo). It's a mystery to me how a rider can tolerate such a devices in a horse's training, and even accept its use at shows.

Key Point: *Many problems, such as poor rideability, resistance, hind leg lameness and much more are often the result of tension-laden "backward riding" and the use of draw reins.*

A demonstration of the effects of draw reins—see the red arrows. It's a mystery to me how any rider can tolerate their use at any time.

A large number of horses that require veterinary help do so simply from being ridden incorrectly! Equestrian federations and organizations should urgently warn against the damaging effects of draw reins in their publications. In fact, the use of draw reins should be prohibited altogether.

Ride outdoors!

As a prerequisite of forwardness, preserve the horse's joy of going by taking it on frequent trail rides. This is particularly true for young horses, but also applies to older ones. Allowing the horse to jump small obstacles outside and climb hills strengthens, and furthers its flexibility and suppleness. It is also much easier to "consolidate" the fourth element of the Training Scale—impulsion—if a horse is ridden out of the arena at times. (Sadly, even though many riders would like to ride their horse out of doors, they don't do so because they are anxious about leaving the security of the indoor arena.)

Impulsion

As mentioned earlier, the term "impulsion" (*Schwung*) is understood quite differently in different areas of the horse world. In my opinion it is often completely misunderstood. On one end of the spectrum there are horses that "run," completely strung-out and unbalanced. They lack "positive" muscle tension in their back and correct "pushing power" from their hind legs (see p. 108). On the other end, and this is the more problematic misinterpretation of impulsion, horses with a tense, rigid back and tight, "passagey" steps are praised and awarded high scores in the dressage ring. Impulsion, in the classical sense, comes from the hind legs. Impulsion is always the result of a systematic strengthening of the extensor muscles, which increases the horse's ability to bend the joints in its haunches. The amount of collection that can be developed is dependant on the amount of impulsion. Impulsion has nothing to do with a tensely held back and a moment of "false"

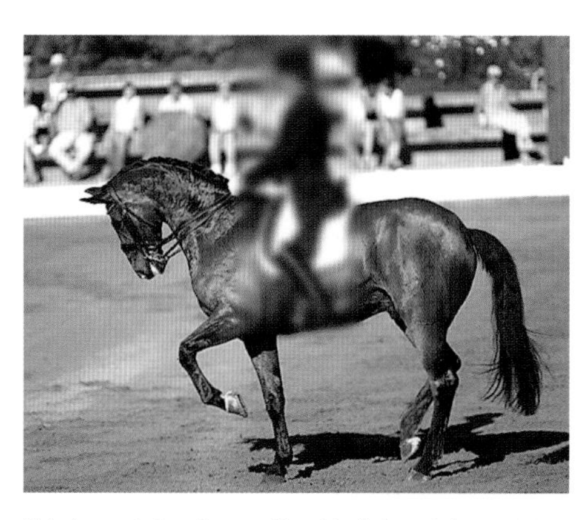

This horse is leaning on the rider's hand, has a tense back, a high croup and no "flexion in the haunches."

A piaffe executed by a horse that's trained according to Classical Principles. The lowered hindquarters carry more weight, which allows the horse to go "uphill." This is example of optimal "flexion in the haunches." The picture shows the self-carriage of a naturally elevated horse[17].

Aus: Schnitzer, 1962/1996

A piaffe executed by a horse that has been worked "from front to back." The elevation that was actively "forced" onto the horse, and the tense back muscle prevent the hind legs from stepping under and producing tense steps instead of real collection[17]. See photos of the piaffe on pp. 110 and 111.

Comparing the results of both training methods[17].

[17] The illustrations were taken from an essay by the same author, "Piaffe without Collection?" published in *Reiter Revue International* No. 5, May 1962. They were used furthermore in the series "Grundsätze der Gymastizierung des Pferdes" ("basics of gymnasticizing the riding horse") published in *Pferdespiegel* No. 5, May 1996. The series; No. 3, 4, 5, 7, 1996 *Pferdespiegel*.

suspension created by trailing hind legs. The so-called "spectacular-looking" trot with expressive front legs followed by "slow" hind legs that we are seeing in competition is physically and psychologically damaging to horses. How can it be that riders demonstrating what were considered training mistakes in the 1950s are highly praised and rewarded today? Where are our organization heads and judging officials when we need them to rein in this chaotic riding?

Developing "pushing power" and collection

In addition to the correct (i.e. *individually* adjusted) positioning of the head-neck axis, the *development of "pushing power"* is another important prerequisite for training a horse correctly.

In order to understand the meaning of the term "pushing power," I'll first explain and analyze the expression "flexion in the haunches." The term can be misleading. You might think that an extreme angling of the hind limbs means that flexion in a horse's haunches is particularly good; this is not the case.

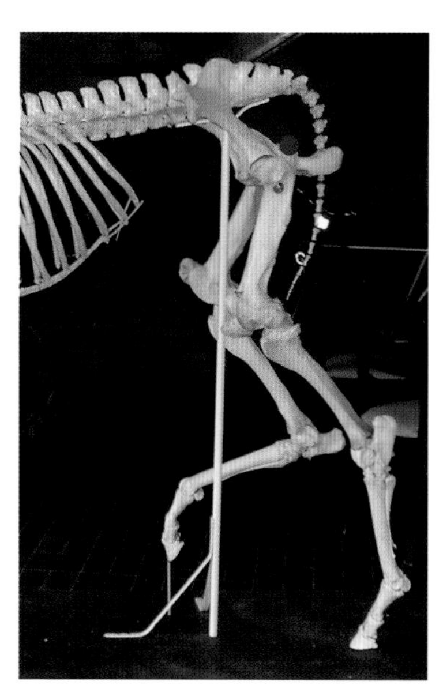

The large joints of the haunches: the hip, stifle and hock. The red circle shows the greater trochanter bone, where the gluteus medius muscle attaches.

The term "haunches" refers to the large joints of the hindquarters: the hip joints, stifles and hocks. The stifles and hocks are connected via a ligamentous apparatus, and are able to flex or extend only when working in synchrony, and for this reason, the hocks are considered part of the haunches.

Let's take a look at a movement cycle of a hind limb at the trot, and see what the correlating muscle action is:

The *"phase of support"* (at the trot, this means the diagonal leg pair contacts the ground) is followed by the *phase of "push-off."* Pushing power develops through the extension of the limbs by extensor muscles. Depending on the tempo or the degree of collection, this happens with more or less energy. What follows is the *"swing phase"*—when a hoof loses contact with the ground as it swings forward through the air. The hind leg is flexed and brought forward. The flexor muscles become active.

For the limbs to be able to touch the ground again, the muscles have to extend again: the extensors are at work. During the phase of support, the extensors have to keep the legs in the desired position. They now have to work to carry the weight of the body.

As the hind limbs extend, there is an angle to both the stifles and the hocks: the larger (flatter) those angles are, that is, the greater the extension of the limbs, the easier it is for the horse to perform.

Key Point: *A horse has "flexion in the haunches" (seen most easily during the support phase of a movement at slower tempos) when it sinks down giving up the larger and more comfortable angles in the hip joints, stifles and hocks. A decrease in these angles allows the horse to push off the ground from this flexed position with greater dynamics, impulsion and loftiness. This is known as collection.*

It's obvious that strenuous "flexing of the haunches" requires a great amount of additional strength from the hind leg extensors. (Just try to walk for a while with bent knee joints!)

IN A NUTSHELL

Signs of a "compressed" horse (ridden from *front to back*):

- Absolute elevation
- Broken neckline
- "Fixed" or hollow back
- High croupa
- Damaged or ruined basic gaits:
  - ambling at the walk
  - disrupted diagonal at the trot ("throwing" the front legs with slow, trailing hind legs)
  - four-beat canter
- Toe-flicking during trot extensions

[18] Neindorff, Egon von, *Die reine Lehre der klassischen Reitkunst* ("the truth about classical horsemanship"), Cadmos Verlag, 2005

[19] Also see Steinbrecht, Gustav, 1995.

The extensor muscles are capable of executing such a performance only when they're adequately strengthened and correctly trained. For this reason, the Classical Principles of riding mainly ask for riding forward in rhythm on large circles and on trails during the first two years of training. Jumping over small obstacles and canter work using the light seat also strengthens the extensor system of the limbs, and with it the horse's "engine."

These days we often see, especially in professional training facilities, how a rider attempts to "shift the horse's weight more onto its hind legs" very early on in its training. Through active hand influence, especially when using draw reins, the rider "fixes" the horse's back muscles through the head-neck position and attempts to develop steps in place although the horse is still young and undeveloped. The result is generally a horse that struggles on the spot without the slightest amount of "flexion in the haunches" or desired uphill movement.

Key Point: *If the rider fails to take the time to consistently strengthen the extensor system of the haunches, it will be impossible to execute movements such as piaffe or passage correctly, even when riding a mature horse.*

Anatomical preconditions of the horse

When buying a horse, ensure that the horse has the necessary anatomical characteristics for the chosen discipline.

Some horses have a straight neck that has little arch to it and riders attempt to curve the head-neck set through hand influence—often with disastrous consequences (see photo for a "well-set" neck).

A horse with an "honest" contact with a supple poll is typically coupled with an elastic, flexible, strong hind leg. "The hind legs bounce back off the rider's back[18]," says Egon von Neindorff. A straight hind leg with little propulsive effect makes it difficult to achieve "flexion in the haunches" and true collection later on. I'd go so far as to say that a stiff hind leg always accompanies a stiff poll lacking suppleness[19].

As a general rule, the following applies: *every horse must be ridden according to its natural anatomy.* The rider should only offer a light, gentle connection and try to achieve steady contact while following the classical Training Scale.

It can take several months until a horse with less favorable anatomy offers a comfortable and soft contact on its own. Longer-bodied, rectangular horses with big gaits full of impulsion tend to tempt the rider to proceed too quickly. Such a modern, big-gaited horse, ridden in absolute elevation quickly becomes a "leg mover," or if ridden with hyperflexion, it will move with an overstretched back. When training such horses one must take constant care to keep the upper neckline stretched forward, ride well forward using a supple (light) seat with the stirrups adjusted not too long. Only when such a back has become stable and carrying, should it be asked to assume more load and influence from the rider. "Old-fashioned" horses bred with a shorter back and shorter legs are not so much at risk. On the other hand, it requires a lot of rider skill to encourage the backs of such horses to swing.

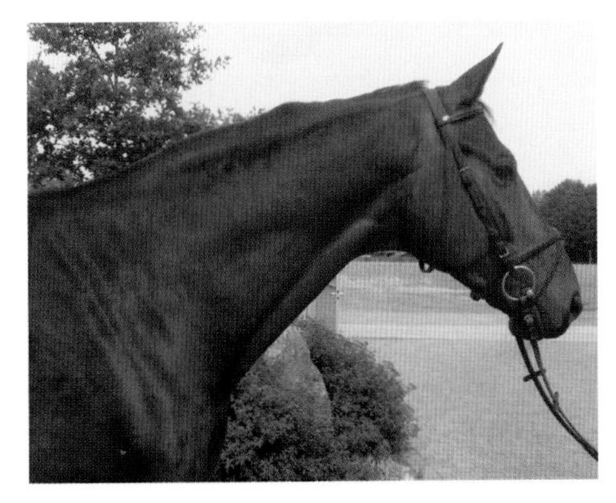

This horse's neck is not set too high on his body, and it has become well muscled through early correct training.

Correct collection—is it still in demand?

The illustration on top of p. 107 shows the silhouette of a horse in piaffe as it's supposed to look according to Classical Training Principles.

Unfortunately, silhouettes seen in today's show rings often look quite different. As explained earlier, correct collection becomes possible when the horse "flexes in the haunches." This only happens if the extensor muscles and the ligament system are allowed to develop over a long period of time with correct training.

A horse whose head and neck outline is fashioned too soon, or with auxiliary reins, never develops the "archer's bow-like" back shape that is formed by positive tension created between the hindquarters and the horse's mouth. Instead, its back is "fixed" or hollow, and the neck muscles are poorly developed. There is a "ditch-like" dip in front of the shoulder blades where the upper neck joins into the withers. Such faulty development doesn't allow the "pushing power"of the hindquarters to flow softly forward toward the horse's mouth.

The picture one most commonly sees these days, shows hindquarters that are

A faulty piaffe with the supporting front leg pushed under the body, the horse "curled-up" behind the vertical, the head-neck axis too deep and the horse not in front of the rider's aids.

relatively sprawled out behind, forelegs that are too far under the body, a high croup, a short neck with a tight throatlatch area, a broken neckline and upper neck muscles with little prominence.

These horses "stamp" during the piaffe, and also often show a disrupted diagonal sequence of footfalls. According to classical philosophy, this movement presented in such a way cannot be called piaffe. More than likely, such horses began their schooling with passage-like steps early on, with the trainer failing to adhere to the classical and correct path of training.

A prolonged phase of suspension created by a "held" or taut back may appear impressive, but has nothing in common with a true passage. It certainly leads to rhythm faults, the loss of the diagonal sequence of footfalls, and all too often also increases the risk of damage in the horse's locomotion apparatus.

An exemplary piaffe! Ideally, the curb rein should have less contact than the snaffle rein.

***Key Point:** Reviewing the quality of these movements enables an expert to determine how the horse was trained. These findings should weigh heavily into the score of a dressage test, and should outweigh the quality of the "technical" rider execution. (See also quote by Erich Glahn, p. 31.)*

***Key Point:** I think that at this point a fundamental question needs to be asked. What is the goal of "modern" dressage training today?*

Is it that everybody just wants to see a spectacular show, which attracts many

QUOTE

> "All movements: lateral, turns, half-halts, full halts develop easily on their own out of correct collection; they certainly serve to increase a horse's flexibility, and improve and refine its training. The reverse, however, is not true: these movements are not able to bring about collection when the horse has not been prepared for it; they are consequences, not causes. When training, what comes first should be the necessary collection; only then the movement, which in turn increases collection." [Quote from *Grundzüge der Reitkunst* ("main features of horsemanship") by Gustav von Dreyhausen, Vienna 1951, p. 15.]

people—including laymen—to the big competitions to watch flashy, musical rides without taking into consideration the method of training behind the excitement produced? Or, should we be rewarding the less showy but more horse-friendly dressage? At the moment, in the dressage "world," there's an attempt on all sides to come up with an odd sort of balancing act. The gist of judges' remarks given in press conferences tell us that official judges in international competitions want to see a "show" in the Grand Prix test; and that Classical Principles are not of interest anymore. So, when will a correctly ridden dressage horse have another opportunity to fairly compete against the "show" mounts" if what is being rewarded is this unrhythmic toe-flicking? I have personally observed the highest score possible –a "10"—awarded to such a "flashy" horse. On the other hand, there is some progress in the opposite direction: the FN's department of training and education runs a campaign about "Better Riding"; the FN's publishing company, FN Verlag, and serious equestrian publishers in the USA and the UK offer numerous valuable books that are dedicated to the principles of the classical art of riding, and the German Riding School trains according to these principles.

Exemplary self-carriage of both horse and rider in the passage. Ideally, the forward-stepping hind leg should be "quicker."

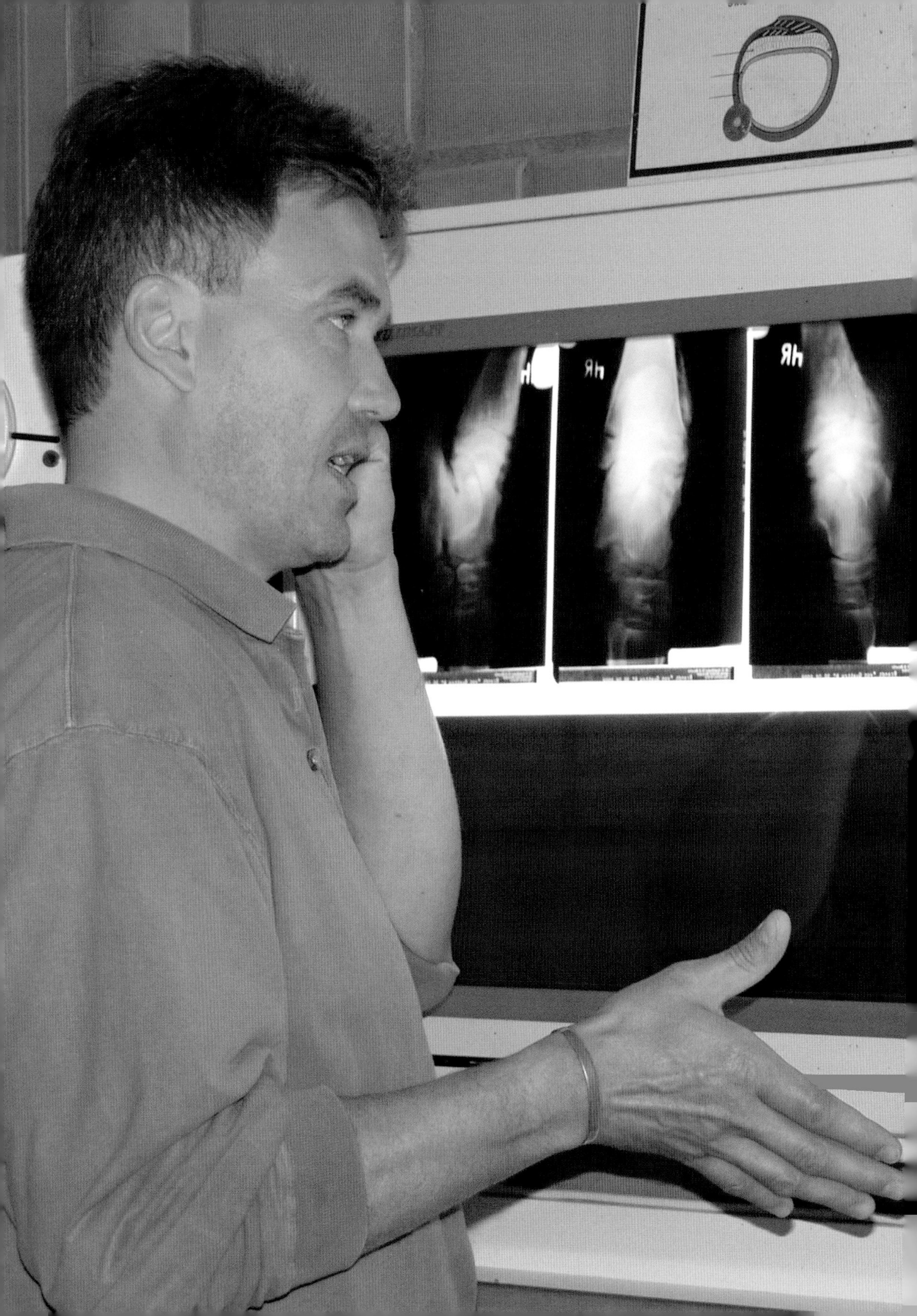

TRAINING FROM A VETERINARY POINT OF VIEW

As a specialist equine veterinarian and *Pferdewirt* (professional rider and trainer who is also trained in horse management) I'm regularly confronted with "patients" showing a multitude of symptoms that can be traced back all too often to incorrect training methods. The riders or owners are often astonished when the cause of lameness or gait anomaly cannot be ascribed to physical diagnostic findings. A lack in ability for self-critical analysis doesn't always make it easy to communicate to a rider that the presented horse is not (yet) injured, but that the rider or trainer has to review, analyze and change his training methods.

The biggest mistakes gravely affecting the horse's health and soundness are made at the beginning of its training, that is, during the phase of the horse's

The author at work.

so-called "basic" training. In the first two years of training, the horse's powerful body undergoes the biggest developmental steps. The term "development" alone communicates to us a central and recurrent claim: in order to train a horse according to Classical Principles, we need time. However, not everybody who is involved in training a young horse takes enough time these days—and this mistake causes most horses to develop locomotion problems, which are presented to veterinarians for diagnosis and resolution.

After 20 years of veterinary practice, and having experienced all the usual successes and failures in diagnosing lameness in a horse, I've expanded my examination methods: during the last 10 years, I've also been doing causal research. I'll explain why: quite often, a veterinarian is presented with a case of lameness where it's impossible to make a definite diagnosis, even with the latest state-of-the-art examination methods.

Why is this? In my view, veterinarians commit a big sin of omission: although we veterinarians intensively examine horses presented to us, and look for the cause of the pain that's causing the lameness, what we often don't do is ask how the patient is used and how he's ridden.

From reading the previous chapters it should have become clear how big an effect a rider with a bad (or good) influence has on his horse, so a veterinarian should not neglect the training background of the horse presented to him. Many movement disturbances and cases of lameness in riding horses are simply a result of improper training. When these equine patients are observed under saddle they almost always show extreme tension, crookedness, and a lack of "throughness." In the past, we commonly referred to this as "rein lameness."

In human medicine it would be unthinkable to proceed in such a way: an orthopedist, for example, must include his patient's sporting interests in his observation. After making a diagnosis, he naturally provides the patient with concrete training advice. It can only be provided, however, if the physician is familiar with the discipline and type of sport his patient pursues.

For an equine orthopedist, this means that in many cases he must go beyond the commonly applied examination methods and examine the horse under saddle, too. The horse should be examined under its usual rider, another rider or the veterinarian himself. I think it's highly important that veterinarians who have

IN A NUTSHELL

Clinical observations

In veterinary practice, horses are often presented for lameness, yet the cause cannot be determined with traditional and supplemental examination methods. In such cases, locomotion problems are often traced back to incorrect training methods. The following is a summary of important clues:

1. Poor or incorrect muscling and signs of physical tension

- Poorly developed upper neck muscle
- Prominent under-neck muscles
- The upper neck shows poor integration into the withers (a dip in front of the shoulder blade)
- Tension in the *longissimus* long back muscles
- Sore *longissimus* muscles
- *Longissimus* muscles that are uneven in height and tone, and showing uneven contraction
- A large, bulky abdomen, indicating poorly developed abdominal muscles
- A tail held high and tensed
- A tail held crookedly

Horses being warmed-up in a hyperflexed manner—in the *Rollkur* position. It shows no respect for the horses, at all.

2. Gait anomalies in movement

Without a rider shown in hand on firm ground

- From no sign of any lameness whatsoever, to...
- Moderate mixed lameness, especially behind

Without a rider on the longe with a halter

- Lameness of various degrees in the hindquarters
- Lameness often changes with longeing direction: generally the inside hind leg is affected, and one side shows more lameness than the other
- Incorrect flexion to the outside of the circle
- During trot, sporadic "hopping" into the canter with the front legs only

Ridden by its usual rider

- The symptoms described above intensify
- The horse's innate crookedness that should be diminishing as training proceeds instead becomes more marked: the lameness might be clearly stronger on one hand (the horse's stiff side) and disappear altogether on the other (the horse' s hollow side)
- The horse is lazy or overly sensitive to the aids
- The horse shows loss of impulsion under the rider as compared to its movement on the longe
- Considerable problems with contact
- The horse shows a general stiffness under the rider
- The natural sequence of the basic gaits is not uniform and rhythmical—the walk is the most sensitive indicator of this

Examination under saddle by veterinarian

- Obvious stiffness
- Extreme crookedness
- Lameness considerably more pronounced on the stiff side
- Short, scurrying walk
- Resistance—to the point of rearing

an interest in horses make an effort to acquire a solid basic education as a rider.

Let's take the cases of a group of young horses, mostly three- to six-year-olds, showing a common pattern of movement: they are lame on the inside leg with the lameness switching to the other inside leg when the direction is changed, especially when ridden.

This lameness is typically caused by tension in the *longissimus* back muscles. Normally, as one hind leg starts to carry the weight at the end of the suspension or swing-phase, the back muscle on the same side contracts, and the muscle on the opposite side relaxes. If the muscles are tense, stiff or sore, the hind leg is not able to adequately swing forward under the body. In order to be able to do that, the back muscle needs to allow maximum stretch, and when the muscle is sore, it is unable to perform that stretch so the leg contacts the ground sooner. With the change of direction the symptoms of this type of lameness shift to the other side.

The commonly seen view from the side of a horse with its front legs spectacularly stretched out as far as possible ("toe-flicking") has become the main criteria for "quality" in young, potential dressage horses as well as in mature animals. A win (or loss) in the show ring, therefore, is not decided by the horse's length of step and development of impulsion, but rather by the showy effect of this trot. This phenomenon caused by hand-dominated training runs through all ranks and levels including the upper echelons of dressage championships. Rhythm faults, swaying, and uneven "short-long" stepping during passage all originate from overuse of the hands and resulting compression of the horse.

Purity of rhythm and soundness in the basic gaits and their further development are not the only aspects that intrinsically depend on the existence of a loose, positively working muscular system. In the broadest sense, I also believe that there's an important relationship between training method and healthy legs. I think that it is necessary to research to what extent the frequency of tendon and ligament injuries (notably the suspensory ligament) and joint problems is more frequent in horses that are worked in tension than in horses that are worked according to Classical Principles. In my opinion, the frequency of suspensory injuries is related to this.

Another example of a horse being ridden in the hyperflexed position—note how much it is on the forehand. In my opinion, horses trained like this experience many more suspensory ligament injuries.

Treatment and correction

After taking appropriate corrective measurements under saddle using the light seat, such as fine-tuning the horse to the leg through leg-yielding, asking it to chew on the bit, trotting on, then later adding in frequent trot-canter transitions or doing work on the longe line or double longe, the symptoms I've mentioned on the preceding pages often improve considerably by themselves, sometimes even disappearing altogether.

As soon as such a horse is brought into a stretching position with its back unburdened, the locomotion disturbances generally resolve.

The procedure becomes more difficult, though not entirely different in nature, when the symptoms described are accompanied by radiographic changes in the thoracic and/or lumbar spine.

In such cases, it can be useful to eliminate or decrease the pain medically in order to bring the horse more quickly into the desired and relieved position with a forward-and-downward stretched head and neck.

Depending on the existence (or non-existence) and the severity of the radiographic findings in the horse's back, or depending on the horse's age, then corrective adjustments in its training can take a few weeks to as long as several months to achieve lasting success. What's often most difficult to achieve during this process is getting the horse's regular rider to make similar adjustments!

For colleagues and therapists who are not skilled equestrians, work on the longe or double longe is a fantastic way to do basic therapeutic work. However, work with the double longe, in particular, calls for thorough initial instruction, consistency and trainer experience. If used incorrectly, longeing, and especially long-lining can be harmful to the horse. The first introduction of long lines can evoke a defensive, fear-based reaction from the horse. The time it takes to properly accustom the horse to long-lining depends on the individual horse. Therefore, one must be extremely careful when introducing this training tool.

This horse is in the beginning steps of piaffe with an overstretched back and neck and a badly sitting rider.

Top: An example of "pseudo-piaffe" according to Udo Bürger's book, *The Way to Perfect Horsemanship*. In the "pseudo-piaffe," the horse nods its head, drops its back, does not lower its croup, and its hind legs trail out behind.
Bottom: A Westfalian gelding demonstrating piaffe wearing a cavesson but no bit.

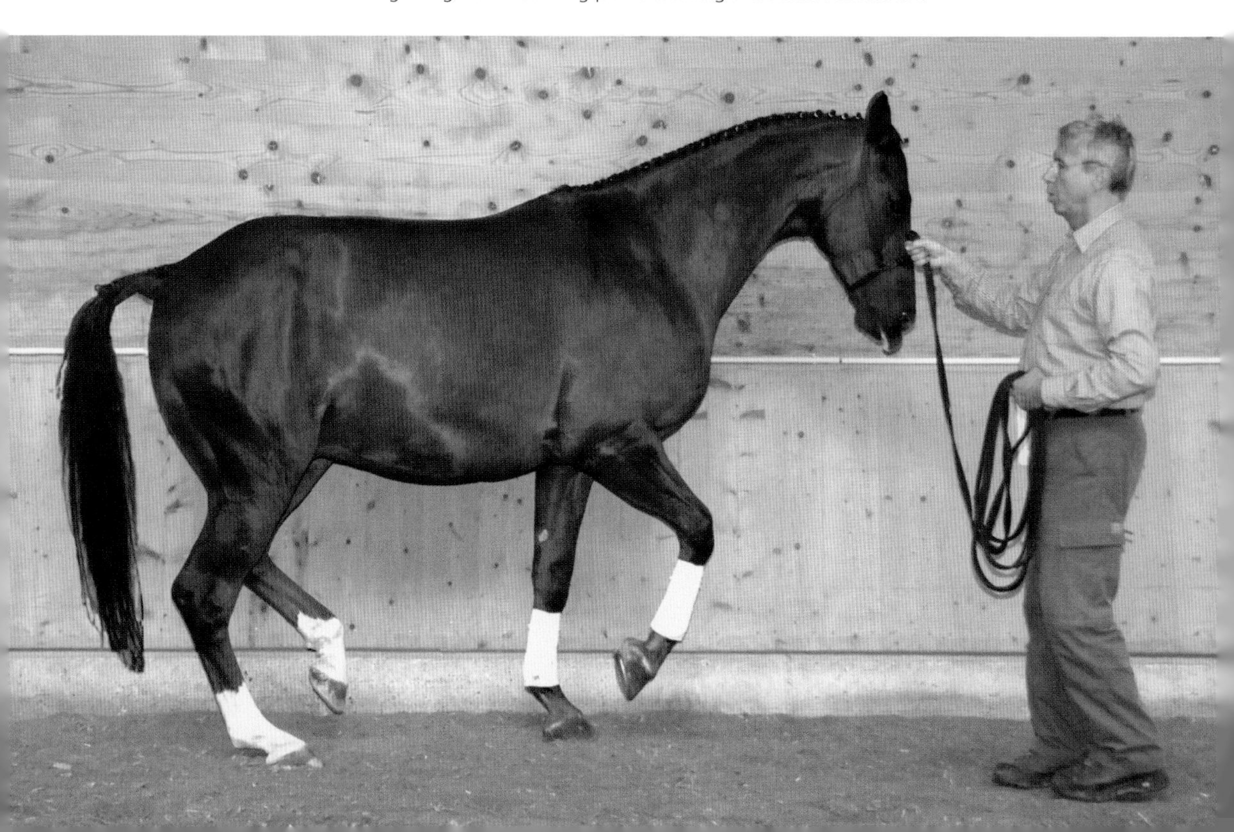

The great importance of looseness (*Losgelassenheit*)

Looseness is a central criterion for a horse's entire training. The sequence of the Training Scale must remain untouched; however, looseness remains the indispensable prerequisite in each training phase, as only through looseness can:

1. The gaits remain "pure"
2. The horse achieve the optimal muscle tone
3. Real collection be achieved
4. Complete "throughness" be attained
5. The horse develop its maximum capacity to perform without getting tired.

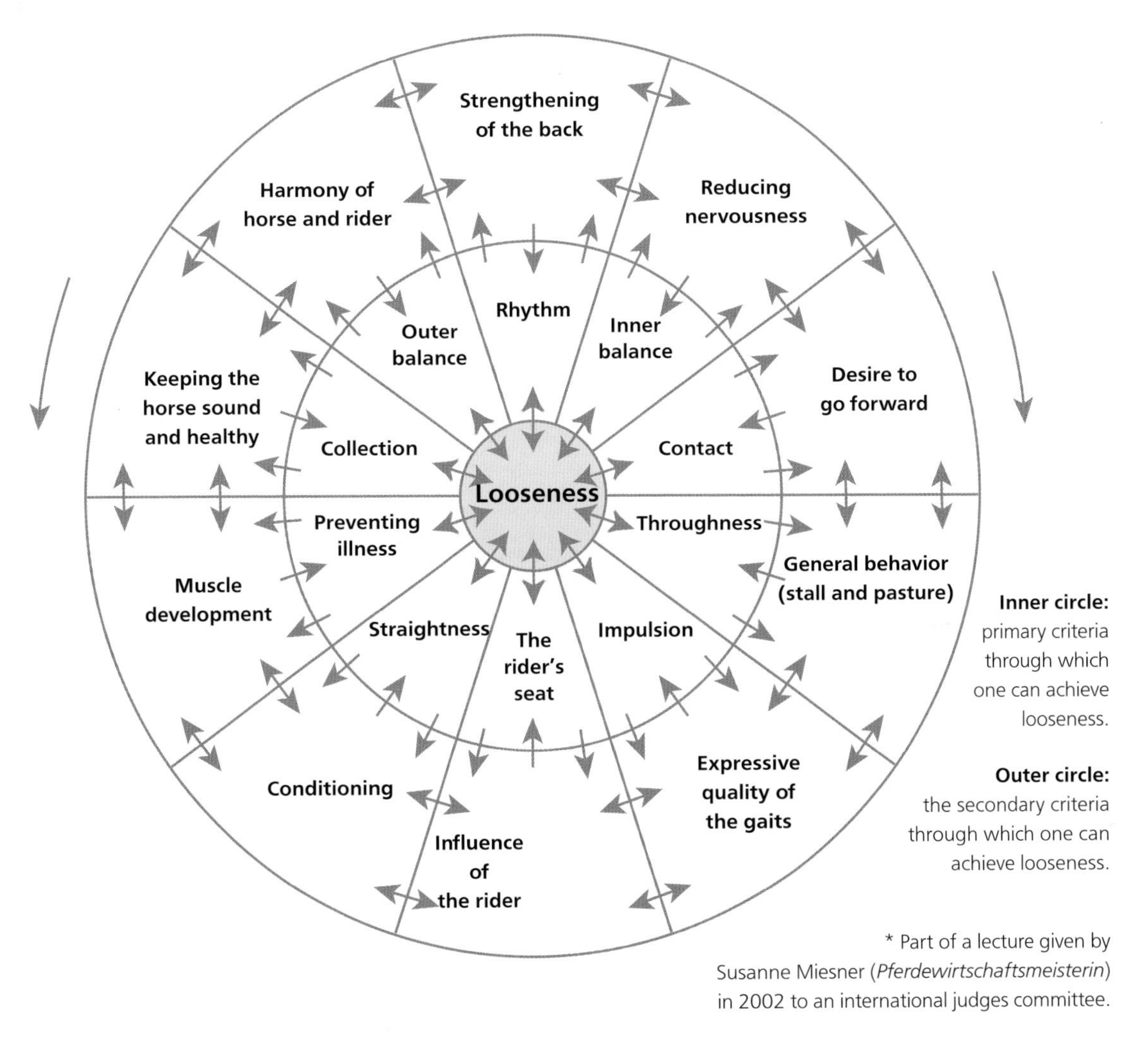

Inner circle: primary criteria through which one can achieve looseness.

Outer circle: the secondary criteria through which one can achieve looseness.

* Part of a lecture given by Susanne Miesner (*Pferdewirtschaftsmeisterin*) in 2002 to an international judges committee.

CONCLUSIONS

To prevent our current mistakes from being repeating in the future, we should attach great importance to adherence to Classical Principles, particularly when training young horses and riders.

I do not understand how, just because someone is a horse enthusiast, he or she is allowed to mount a horse without having any previous education whatsoever, and calls himself or herself a "rider" from that very moment on. Imagine this approach applied to the sport of hang gliding or diving! And, such disciplines do not involve another living individual creature that, on the one hand, is very strong, yet on the other, very delicate and sensitive.

Isn't it time to couple a person's introduction to equestrian sport by a professional with a solid theoretical and practical education, for the well-being of our horses? Such a basic education should include theory and practice regarding how to behave around horses as well as provide a look into the horse's physiology, conformation and behavior. Instructors should convey to their students that riding a horse means more than merely "sitting on it."

Revision of the basic education of riders is not the only thing that needs to be addressed; the testing system of young horses is also in need of fundamental modification. One thing is certain: a three-year-old horse, for example, has no busi-

Three examples of young horses being trained piaffe in hand correctly. Note the handler is using a cavesson only—no bit. You can really see the exemplary uphill position and use of "flexion in the haunches."

ness regularly attending shows. At best, and only in exceptional cases, should a youngster be shown at such venues and then only one that is specifically designed to accommodate the nature of a young horse. Also, a young horse should not be permitted to show in a dressage saddle—turning a horse into a specialist in its discipline should begin only after two years of basic ridden training.

It would also be desirable to reestablish the relationship between outdoor riding and elementary tests. The training and testing of young riders as well as young horses should show versatility during the first two years.

Key Point: *As I said earlier, never before have there been so many riders, such good quality riding horses, such fantastic organizations, and capital available for funding in the equestrian sports as there are today. If we could only manage to train and test all horses according to old, time-proven and animal-friendly principles, our sport will become the most beautiful of all.*

QUOTE

"Dressage riding certainly is the hardest of all arts requiring patient preparation and training over many years to reach the highest levels, which when attained, the horse can only perform at for a few years. Nonetheless, it is the most noble of arts because you mold and train a living creature, spend a long time tolerating each other's character faults, and then the horse becomes your most reliable and most loyal friend." [Quote from *Anleitung zur Dressur und Ausbildung des Pferdes* ("manual of dressage and development of the horse") by Julius Walzer, Olms Verlag, 2004.]

Closing words

Like me, an increasing number of riders long to see a way of riding that doesn't restrain, is natural and relaxed, and where the focus remains on classical training principles, not show and spectacle, which has been produced in a manner that is detrimental to the horse's well-being.

Now that the economic aspect has become an inherent part of the horse industry, I believe that the judges bear more responsibility than ever to make sure this happens! In the future, it is my hope that independent judges, confident in their own opinions, will consistently apply the universally valid, time-proven and irrevocable classical system as the foundation for their decisions, and that they are willing to represent this philosophy without compromise.

Instructors, of course, play a big role in this. For many trainers and instructors it must be very hard, I'm sure, to convey Classical Principles to young people if the trainers themselves have violated these principles for many years—often for economic reasons or pressures to succeed.

Because riders have become accustomed to seeing tightly strapped mouths and twisted necks manipulated by draw reins, it sadly has become difficult to imagine our riding facilities without them. As you can see in the picture on p. 45, even our youngest riders already imitate these terrible training methods.

Key Point: *A horse's body needs* ***time*** *to develop, just as a human body does in order to become an athlete; this concept must re-enter our awareness.*

A piaffe showing good self-carriage and a nicely sitting rider. However, the hind legs could be more active and the horse's back is tense (as shown by the tail position). The horse should collect from the rider's seat, but here the curb rein is used instead.

I'm well aware that this is not easy in the fast-paced times in which we live. However, I envision one approach that can tackle the problem at its roots and that is in the design of tests for young horses. For three-year-olds, the number of times they are shown per season should be limited. As I said before, dressage saddles should not be on the backs of these youngsters. There is great value in presenting such horses by riding them with the light seat (see p. 96) and without tension. Bridles should be examined, as well, in order to abolish the fashion of tight nosebands being used so mercilessly and so mindlessly.

Young horses whose head and neck set has been created with force and hands should be penalized or eliminated, as should those showing piaffe and passage before they are truly ready; the Training Scale should determine the progression of training.

Please reflect on the following—why is it so difficult to act ethically?

When the publication *Ethische Grundsätze des Pferdefreundes* ("Ethical Principles for the True Horseman") was published in 1994 by the German National Equestrian Federation (FN) nobody imagined that within 10 years more than 100,000 copies would be sold. To this day, there have been seven editions of this booklet printed.

The Nine Ethical Principles of the True Horseman

1. Anyone involved with a horse takes over responsibility for this living creature entrusted to him.
2. The horse must be kept in a way that is in keeping with its natural living requirements.
3. Highest priority must be accorded to the physical as well as psychological health of the horse, irrespective of the purpose for which it is used.
4. Man must respect every horse alike, regardless of its breed, age and sex and its use for breeding, for recreation or in sporting competition.
5. Knowledge of the history of the horse, its needs, and how to handle it are part of our historic-cultural heritage. This information must be cherished and safeguarded in order to be passed on to the next generations.
6. Contact and dealings with horses are character-building experiences and of valuable significance to the development of the human being—in particular, the young person. This aspect must always be respected and promoted.

7. The human who participates in equestrian sport with his horse must subject himself, as well his horse to training. The goal of any training is to bring about the best possible harmony between rider and horse.
8. The use of the horse in competition as well as in general riding, driving and vaulting must be geared toward the horse's ability, temperament and willingness to perform. Manipulating a horse's capacity to work by means of medication or other "horse-unfriendly" influences should be rejected by all and people engaged in such practices should be prosecuted.
9. The responsibility a human has for the horse entrusted to him includes the end of the horse's life. The human must always assume this responsibility and implement any decisions in the best interest of the horse.

The author and the publishers are always dismayed to discover that these ethical guidelines are all too often ignored. Perhaps it is because people just don't know about them or understand their meaning. We hope that the book *Tug of War* provides a broad explanation for the reasons behind the Nine Ethical Principles and that readers and their horses will enjoy the benefits of practical application.

AFTERWORD

An Acknowledgement and a Note of Encouragement

I take my hat off to all people who have the courage to stand up, not follow the crowd, at times be "loud" and clearly point out deplorable states of affairs. This is especially true when they have suggestions about how to solve the difficult issues that affect our horses such as are described in this book (which also illustrates ways to solve dilemmas riders face today).

Horses don't have a sound for expressing pain. Just imagine how loud the noise would be in many a warm-up arena at both big and small equestrian competitions if these wonderful creatures opened their mouths not only when facing a hand that is too hard...

Gerd Heuschmann is their voice! He hardly ever minces words—even when all sides have been trying to persuade him that he'd be better off proceeding in a more conformist, "politically correct" manner.

At this point I want to say thank you to Gerd and all the people who don't just silently watch, or even run away when they see and hear a horse "cry." The eyes of the horses speak volumes...

So I also ask *you* to speak up if you cannot bear what you might see in a few hours at your barn or in the show ring, or wherever your path might cross horses. Please also encourage the people who already do a good job with their horses to go more public with their methods. I know of many "searching" riders, who have been looking for a good instructor in vain.

Please also support the efforts of individual persons or riding clubs who are advocates of the Classical Principles of riding, and are working to preserve and further them. These many big and small efforts carried by the deep desire to see horses be really "brilliant" in public performances will soon bear fruit.

We owe it to horses to return their dignity to them.

I'm very much looking forward to hearing from you if you also feel you'd like to make the horse world move "in this direction."

One more thing—the golden rule: TIME is what the horse needs most and your patience is the most precious gift you can give.

Isabella Sonntag, Publisher of the German edition of *Tug of War*
Schondorf/Lake Ammersee, September 1, 2006
www.wu-wei-verlag.com

BIBLIOGRAPHY AND RECOMMENDED READING

Albrecht, Kurt, *A Dressage Judge's Handbook,* New Edition, Sydney R. Smith Sporting Books, 1989.

Baucher, François, *A Method of Horsemanship Founded Upon New Principles,* Scholarly Publishing Office, University of Michigan Library, 2006.

Beran Anja, *Classical Schooling with the Horse in Mind*, Trafalgar Square Books, 2007.

Bürger, Udo, *The Way to Perfect Horsemanship*, Trafalgar Square Books, 1998.

Bürger, Udo, and Otto Zietzschmann, *The Rider Forms the Horse*, New Edition, FN-Verlag, Warendorf, 2004.

Bürkner, Felix, *Ein Reiterleben* ("the equestrian life"), Olms Verlag, 2004.

German National Equestrian Federation (FN), *The Principles of Riding,* Half Halt Press, 1997.

German National Equestrian Federation (FN)/German Olympic Committee for Riding, e.V. (DOKR) (publ.) Jahresbericht (2005), Warendorf/Ostbevern (2006).

Glahn, Erich, *Reitkunst am Scheideweg* ("horsemanship at the crossroads"), Heidenheim, 1956.

HDV 12, *(Reitvorschrift (R.B) vom 18.8.1937 H. Dv. 12–*"riding regulations of 1912"), Verlag Mittler & Sohn, 2001.

Mossdorf, Carl Friedrich, *Kavallerieschule Hannover* ("the cavalry school of Hanover"), 3rd ed., FN-Verlag, Warendorf, 1989.

Nickel, Richard, A. Schummer, and E. Seiferle, *Lehrbuch der Anatomie des Haustieres* ("textbook of the anatomy of domestic animals"), vol. 1-5, 5th ed., Blackwell-Wissensch Verlag, 1982.

Racinet, Jean C., *Racinet Explains Baucher,* Xenophon Press, 1997.

Schnitzer, Ulrich, "Grundsätze deer Gymnastizierung des Pferdes" ("the basics of gymnasticizing the riding horse"), *PferdeSpiegel,* 1996.

Steinbrecht, Gustav, *The Gymnasium of the Horse*, Xenophon Press, 1995.

Stensbeck, Oscar M., and Gustav von Dreyhausen, *Grundzüge der Reitkunst* ("main features of horsemanship"), Olms Verlag, 2004.

Stodulka, Dr. med. Vet. Robert, *Medizinische Reitlehre* ("medical riding lessons"), Parey Verlag, 2006.

von Neindorff, Egon, *Die reine Lehre der klassischen Reitkunst* ("the truth about classical horsemanship"), Cadmos Verlag, 2004.

von Redwitz, Max Freiherr, *Die Grundsätze der Dressur* ("principles of dressage"), Aachen, 1987.

Recommended Web Sites

www.drv-online.de
www.fn-dokr.de
www.fn-handbuch.de
www.pferd-aktuell.de
www.fn-verlag.de
www.anjaberan.de
www.horsesport.org
www.classical-dressage.net
www.sustainabledressage.net
www.spanishridingschool.com
www.xenophon-classical-riding.org
http://nicholnl.wcp.muohio.edu/dingosBreakfastClub/biomech/longandlow.html
www.hippocampus.nl.com
www.reitkunst.com
www.von-neindorff-stiftung.de
www.horsesforlife.com

PHOTO CREDITS

Photos:

Archives: 4, 20, 22, 24, 26, 32, 34 *top*, 39, 51 *left*, 56, 58 *top*, 59, 61 *bottom*, 77, 78, 79 *top*, 81, 82, 98, 103, 122 *top*, 126

Private: 18, 67, 89, 91, 92, 93, 101 *top*, 106, 108, 111, 117, 120, 121

Alexandra Gräfin Dohna: 46 *left*

Ramona Dünisch: 45

Uta Helkenberg: 114

Gerd Heuschmann: 42, 47, 48, 49, 50, 55, 101 *bottom*, 102, 105

Sven Kramer: 89

Jürgen Richter: 94

Holger Schupp: 29, 61 *top*, 104

Jacques Toffi: 51

Stefan Wartini: 46 *right*, 58 *bottom*, 62, 70, 73, 79 *bottom*, 99, 100 *right*, 110, 122 *bottom*

Hilde Weeg: 17

Maximilian Schreiner: 61 *top*, 86, 106 *left*, 113

Guillaume Levesque: 90, 91

From *The Rider Forms the Horse* by Udo Bürger and Otto Zietzschmann, courtesy of FN-Verlag, Warendorf: 113

From *Dressurreiten* by Richard L. Wätjen, courtesy of Paul Parey Verlag: 36

The photographer for this photograph could not be contacted (courtesy of Jacques Toffi/FN-Archiv, from *Deutsche Reiterliche Vereinigung: FN-Handbuch Pferdewirt,* FN-Verlag, Warendorf): 34 *bottom*

Drawings by:

Kaja Möbius

INDEX

Page numbers in *italic* indicate illustrations or photographs:

INDEX

INDEX